CREATIVE
COMMONS

for **Educators** *and* **Librarians**

CREATIVE COMMONS

for **Educators** *and* **Librarians**

CREATIVE COMMONS

ALA
Editions

CHICAGO 2020

ISBN: 978-0-8389-1946-0 (paper)

Library of Congress Cataloging-in-Publication Data
Names: Creative Commons (Organization), author.
Title: Creative commons for educators and librarians / Creative Commons.
Description: Chicago : ALA Editions, 2020. | Includes bibliographical references and index. | Summary: "The authoritative source for learning about using creative commons licenses and advocating for their use in your academic community"— Provided by publisher.
Identifiers: LCCN 2019027187 | ISBN 9780838919460 (paperback)
Subjects: LCSH: Copyright licenses—United States. | Creative Commons (Organization), | Library copyright policies—United States.
Classification: LCC KF3002 .C74 2019 | DDC 346.7304/82—dc23
LC record available at https://lccn.loc.gov/2019027187

Cover design by Alex Diaz. Cover image, "Circles" by Asitha De Silva, is a work in the public domain. Available from Flickr: flickr.com/photos/131715569@N03/20164473614.

⊚ This paper meets the requirements of ANSI/NISO Z39.48-1992 (Permanence of Paper).

Printed in the United States of America

24 23 22 21 20   5 4 3 2 1

Contents

1   What Is Creative Commons?   1

2   Copyright Law   13

3   Anatomy of a CC License   39

4   Using CC Licenses and CC-Licensed Works   61

Preface

IN 2001, AT A TIME WHEN TEXTS WERE EXPENSIVE AND VIDEO ON THE WEB was a far-off dream, Creative Commons (CC) began as a rejection of the expansion of copyright. In 1998, Congress passed an Act that extended the term of existing copyrights by twenty years in the United States. This 1998 extension was challenged by CC's founder, Lawrence Lessig, all the way to the Supreme Court, but the Court upheld the Act. In reaction to this decision, a small group of lawyers, academics, and culture activists got together to try to make it easy, simple, and free to share your works on the burgeoning communications platforms of the Internet.

They couldn't change copyright law, so they hacked it. Our founders created a release valve, built on top of the international laws and treaties that govern copyright.

I think it's fair to say that no one knew just how successful the CC licenses would be, or how much we would need them as we entered a world where every single person could be not only a creator, but also a creator of high-quality, reusable content. The seeds of Creative Commons were planted long before social media, before ubiquitous smartphones and broadband access, and before user-generated content platforms. But these seeds set down an essential root in the open Internet, and offered a powerful tool used by individuals, governments, NGOs, and corporations to create, share, and remix content.

Today, there are more than 1.6 billion CC-licensed works hosted on over 9 million websites—including some of the most popular sites on the web. The CC licenses operate in every country and have been translated into more than 30 languages by communities in more than 85 countries. They have been used to share every type of content, from photos and videos to 3D models and datasets.

The CC license tools are now the global standard for sharing of works for use and reuse. From *Wikipedia*, to open access to research and journals, to open education, to open data, these license tools are an essential element of a more equitable and accessible knowledge commons.

Our goal at Creative Commons is to build a vibrant, usable commons of creativity and knowledge, powered by collaboration and gratitude. By default, copyright applies to all original content, so sharing under a copyright license is always a choice. This means we need to help people understand their options, and how they can use the CC licensing tools to maximum benefit. To do this, we need people all around the world to be experts in using, contributing to, and sharing the commons and the open licensing tools that unlock its full potential.

We know that the best way to help others is to give them the knowledge they need to help themselves. And we know that CC's greatest power is sharing—of knowledge, of culture, and of understanding across cultures and communities—so for the first time, we literally wrote the book on Creative Commons, and we are sharing it with everyone. *Creative Commons for Educators and Librarians* is a publication of the CC Certificate course content. The CC Certificate is about investing in people like you: educators, practitioners, creators, open advocates, and activists all over the world. You're the ones who everyday help people make the choice to share and unleash their content so that everyone can benefit from it. That's why we created the CC Certificate course, it's why we're working with our communities to translate the course content and train new leaders to teach it in local languages, and it's why we've made all the content openly accessible under CC BY—to unlock new uses we haven't imagined yet.

We hope this book will help us get a little closer to that goal, and perhaps help us to grow the global community of experts, and ultimately our collective power, through shared knowledge and culture.

Ryan Merkley
CEO, Creative Commons (2014–2019)

Acknowledgments

THE CREATIVE COMMONS CERTIFICATE CONTENT AND THIS PUBLICATION were made possible by the generous support of the following foundations, and the efforts of many partner organizations and individuals:

We gratefully acknowledge the contribution of the Bill & Melinda Gates Foundation, the Samuel H. Kress Foundation, and the William and Flora Hewlett Foundation. This project was also made possible in part by the Institute of Museum and Library Services RE-00-15-0116-15.

Creative Commons is honored to have been able to work with a stellar group of organizations and individuals that contributed to the creation, revision, and refinement of the CC Certificate content and course design, including the American Library Association; the Association of College and Research Libraries; Canvas LMS by Instructure; Hypothes.is; LOUIS Libraries; the Open Textbook Network; and Pressbooks; as well as the international CC legal community, the CC Board of Directors, CC staff, CC Certificate facilitators, and CC Certificate graduates and participants. Visit https://certificates.creativecommons.org/about/acknowledgements/ for a list of associated names.

List of Creative Commons Licenses

THE FIGURES USED THROUGHOUT THIS BOOK ARE CC-LICENSED WORKS OR are available in the public domain. The list below includes the URLs for each CC license or public domain tool referenced in the figures, so you can easily navigate to the appropriate license.

- CC0 1.0 (CC0 1.0 Universal Public Domain Dedication): https://creative commons.org/publicdomain/zero/1.0/
- CC BY 2.0 (Attribution 2.0 Generic): https://creativecommons.org/licenses/by/2.0/
- CC BY 3.0 (Attribution 3.0 Unported): https://creativecommons.org/licenses/by/3.0/
- CC BY 4.0 (Attribution 4.0 International): https://creativecommons.org/licenses/by/4.0/
- CC BY-SA 3.0 (Attribution-ShareAlike 3.0 Unported): https://creative commons.org/licenses/by-sa/3.0/
- CC BY-SA 4.0 (Attribution-ShareAlike 4.0 International): https://creative commons.org/licenses/by-sa/4.0/
- CC BY-NC 4.0 (Attribution-NonCommercial 4.0 International): https://creativecommons.org/licenses/by-nc/4.0/
- CC BY-NC-SA 4.0 (Attribution-NonCommercial-ShareAlike 4.0 International): https://creativecommons.org/licenses/by-nc-sa/4.0/
- CC BY-ND 4.0 (Attribution-NoDerivatives 4.0 International): https://creativecommons.org/licenses/by-nd/4.0/
- CC BY-NC-ND 4.0 (Attribution-NonCommercial-NoDerivatives 4.0 International): https://creativecommons.org/licenses/by-nc-nd/4.0/

1

What Is Creative Commons?

CREATIVE COMMONS IS A SET OF LEGAL TOOLS, A NONPROFIT ORGANIZATION, a global network and a movement—all inspired by people's willingness to share their creativity and knowledge, and enabled by a set of open copyright licenses.

Creative Commons began in response to an outdated global copyright legal system. CC licenses are built on copyright and are designed to give more options to creators who want to share. Over time, the role and value of Creative Commons have expanded. This chapter will introduce you to where Creative Commons came from and where it is headed.

This chapter has three sections:

1. The Story of Creative Commons
2. Creative Commons Today
3. Additional Resources

 Completing the Creative Commons Certificate does not entitle learners to provide legal advice on copyright, fair use/fair dealing, or open licensing. The content in this book and the information that Certificate facilitators share in the Creative Commons course is also not legal advice. While you should not share legal advice with others based on this book's content, you will develop a high level of expertise upon completion of this book. You will learn a lot about copyright, open licensing, and open practices in various communities. Upon finishing this book, you should feel comfortable sharing the facts about copyright and open licensing, case studies, and good open practices.

1.1 | THE STORY OF CREATIVE COMMONS

To understand how a set of copyright licenses could inspire a global movement, you need to know a bit about the origin of Creative Commons (CC).

LEARNING OUTCOMES
- Retell the story of why Creative Commons was founded
- Identify the role of copyright law in the creation of Creative Commons

THE BIG QUESTION: WHY IT MATTERS
What were the legal and cultural reasons for the founding of Creative Commons? Why has CC grown into a global movement?

Creative Commons' founders recognized the mismatch between what technology enables and what copyright restricts, and in response they have provided an alternative approach for creators who want to share their work with others. Today this approach is used by millions of creators around the globe.

PERSONAL REFLECTION: WHY IT MATTERS TO YOU
When did you first learn about Creative Commons? Think about how you would articulate what CC is to someone who has never heard of it. To fully understand the organization, it helps to start with a bit of history.

Acquiring Essential Knowledge

The story of Creative Commons begins with copyright. You'll learn a lot more about copyright later in this book, but for now it's enough to know that copyright is an area of law that regulates the way the products of human creativity are used—products like books, academic research articles, music, and art. Copyright grants a set of exclusive rights to a creator, so that the creator has the ability to prevent others from copying and adapting their work for a limited time. In other words, copyright law strictly regulates who is allowed to copy and share with whom.

The Internet has given us the opportunity to access, share, and collaborate on human creations (all governed by copyright) at an unprecedented scale. But the sharing capabilities made possible by digital technology are in tension with the sharing restrictions embedded within copyright laws around the world.

Creative Commons was created to help address the tension between creators' ability to share digital works globally and copyright regulation. The story begins with a particular piece of copyright legislation in the United States. It was called the Sonny Bono Copyright Term Extension Act (CTEA), and it was enacted in 1998. This Act extended the term of copyright protection for every work in the United States—even those already published—for an additional 20 years, so that the copyright term equaled the life of the creator plus 70 years. (This move put the U.S. copyright term in line with some other countries, though the term in many more countries remains at 50 years after the creator's death to this day.)

(Fun fact: The CTEA was commonly referred to as the Mickey Mouse Protection Act because the extension came just before the original Mickey Mouse cartoon, *Steamboat Willie*, would have fallen into the public domain.)

Stanford University law professor Lawrence Lessig (figure 1.1) believed that this new law was unconstitutional. The term of copyright had been continually extended over the years. The end of a copyright term is important—it marks the moment when a work moves into the public domain, whereupon everyone can use that work for any purpose without permission. This is a critical part of the equation in the copyright system. All creativity and knowledge build on what came before, and the end of a copyright term ensures that copyrighted works eventually move into the public domain and thus join the pool of knowledge and creativity from which we can all freely draw to create new works.

The 1998 law was also hard to align with the purpose of copyright as it is written into the U.S. Constitution—to create an incentive for authors to share their works by granting them a limited monopoly over them. *How could the law possibly further incentivize sharing works that already existed?*

Lessig represented a web publisher, Eric Eldred, who had made a career of making works available as they passed into the public domain. Together, they challenged the consti-

FIGURE 1.1 **Larry Lessig giving #CCSummit2011 keynote**

Photo from Flickr: flickr.com/photos/ dtkindler/6155457139/ Author: DTKindler | CC BY 2.0 Desaturated from original

tutionality of the Act. The case, known as *Eldred vs. Ashcroft*, went all the way to the U.S. Supreme Court. Eldred lost, and the Act was upheld.

Enter Creative Commons

Inspired by the value of Eldred's goal of making more creative works freely available on the Internet, and in response to a growing community of bloggers who were creating, remixing, and sharing content, Lessig and others came up with an idea. They created a nonprofit organization called Creative Commons and, in 2002, they published the Creative Commons licenses—a set of free, public licenses that would allow creators to keep their copyrights while sharing their works on more flexible terms than the default "all rights reserved" approach. Copyright is automatic, whether you want it or not; the moment an original work is fixed in tangible form, it is protected by copyright. And while some people want to reserve all of the rights to their works, many others want to share their works with the public more freely. The idea behind CC licensing was to create an easy way for creators who wanted to share their works in ways that were consistent with copyright law.

From the start, Creative Commons licenses were intended to be used by creators all over the world. The CC founders were initially motivated by a piece of U.S. copyright legislation, but similar copyright laws all over the world restricted how our shared culture and collective knowledge could be used, even while digital technologies and the Internet have opened new ways for people to participate in culture and knowledge production. Since Creative Commons was founded, much has changed in the way people share and how the Internet operates. In many places around the world, the restrictions on using creative works have increased. Yet sharing and remix are now the norm online. Think about your favorite video mashup, or even the photos your friend posted on social media last week. Sometimes these types of sharing and remix happen in violation of copyright law, and sometimes they happen within social media networks that don't allow those works to be shared on other parts of the web.

 Watch the short video *A Shared Culture* by Jesse Dylan to get a sense for the vision behind Creative Commons. **https://creative commons.org/about/videos/a-shared-culture** | CC BY-NC-SA 3.0

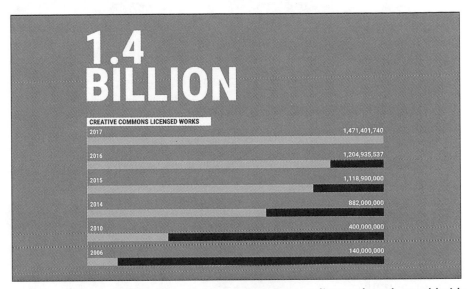

FIGURE 1.2 **Growth in the number of Creative Commons-licensed works worldwide**

In domains like textbook publishing, academic research, documentary film-making, and many other fields, restrictive copyright rules continue to inhibit the creation, access, and remix of works. CC tools are helping to solve this problem. In 2017, CC licenses were used by more than 1.4 billion works online across 9 million websites (figure 1.2); since 2017, the number of CC-licensed works has increased to over 1.6 billion. The grand experiment that started more than fifteen years ago has been a success, sometimes in ways that were unimagined by CC's founders. (For more information, see the "State of the Commons" at the Creative Commons website: https://stateof.creativecommons.org.) While other custom open copyright licenses have been developed in the past, we recommend using Creative Commons licenses because they are up-to-date, free to use, and have been broadly adopted by governments, institutions, and individuals as the global standard for open copyright licenses.

In the next section, you'll learn more about what Creative Commons looks like today—the licenses, the organization, and the movement.

Final Remarks

Technology now makes it possible for online content to be consumed by millions of people at once, and it can be copied, shared, and remixed with speed and ease. But copyright law places limits on our ability to take advantage of these possibilities. Creative Commons was founded to help us realize the full potential of the Internet.

1.2 | CREATIVE COMMONS TODAY

As a set of legal tools, a nonprofit organization, and a global network and movement, Creative Commons has evolved in many ways over the course of its history.

LEARNING OUTCOMES
- Differentiate between Creative Commons as a set of licenses, a movement, and a nonprofit organization
- Explain the role of the CC Global Network
- Describe the basic areas of work for Creative Commons as a nonprofit organization

THE BIG QUESTION: WHY IT MATTERS
Now we know why Creative Commons was started. But what is Creative Commons today?

Today CC licenses are prevalent across the web and are used by creators around the world for every type of content you can imagine. The open movement, which extends beyond just CC licenses, is a global force of people committed to the idea that the world is better when we share and work together. Creative Commons is the nonprofit organization that stewards the CC licenses and helps support the open movement.

PERSONAL REFLECTION: WHY IT MATTERS TO YOU
When you think about Creative Commons, do you think about its licenses? Or about activists seeking copyright reform? A useful tool for sharing? Symbols in circles? Something else?

In addition to giving creators more choices for how to share their work, CC legal tools serve important policy goals in fields like scholarly publishing and education. Watch the brief video *Why Open Education Matters* to get a sense of the opportunities that CC licenses create for education. **https://www.youtube.com/watch?v=gJWbVt 2Nc-I** | CC BY 3.0

Are you involved with Creative Commons as a creator, a reuser, or an advocate? Would you like to be one of these?

Acquiring Essential Knowledge

Today, the CC licenses and public domain tools are used on more than 1.6 billion works, from songs to YouTube videos to scientific research. The licenses have helped a global movement come together around openness, collaboration, and shared human creativity. Creative Commons, the nonprofit organization, was once housed within the basement of the Stanford Law School, but now has a staff working around the world on a host of different projects in various domains.

We'll take these different aspects of Creative Commons—the legal tools, the movement, and the organization—and look at each in turn.

CC LICENSES

CC licenses are legal tools that function as an alternative for creators who choose to share their works with the public under more permissive terms than the default "all rights reserved" approach under copyright. These legal tools are integrated into user-generated content platforms like YouTube, Flickr, and Jamendo, and they are used by nonprofit open projects like *Wikipedia* and Open-Stax. They are also used by formal institutions like the Metropolitan Museum of Art and Europeana, and by millions of individual creators.

Collectively, the CC legal tools help create a global commons of diverse types of content that is freely available for anyone to use. CC licenses may additionally serve a non-copyright function. In communities of shared practices, the licenses act to signal a set of values and a different way of operating.

For some users, this means looking back to the economic model of the commons. As the economist David Bollier describes it, "a *commons* arises whenever a given community decides it wishes to manage a resource in a collective manner, with special regard for equitable access, use and sustainability."[1] *Wikipedia* is a good example of a commons-based community around CC-licensed content.

For a creative take on Creative Commons and copyright, listen to this song by Jonathan "Song-A-Day" Mann about his choice to use CC licenses for his music in *Won't Lock It Down.* **https://www.youtube.com/watch?v=NUGP-oW4_ZE** | CC BY 3.0

For others, the CC legal tools and their icons express an affinity for a set of core values. CC icons have become ubiquitous symbols for sharing, openness, and human collaboration. The CC logo and icons are now part of the permanent design collection at the Museum of Modern Art in New York City.

While there is no single motivation for using CC licenses, there is a basic sense that CC licensing is rooted in a fundamental belief that knowledge and creativity are the building blocks of our culture rather than simple commodities from which to extract market value. The licenses reflect a belief that everyone has something to contribute, and that no one can own our shared culture. Fundamentally, the licenses reflect a belief in the promise and benefits of sharing.

THE MOVEMENT

Since 2001, a global coalition of people has formed around Creative Commons and open licensing.[2] This includes activists working on copyright reform around the globe; policy-makers advancing policies that mandate open access to publicly funded educational resources, research, and data; and creators who share a core set of values. In fact, most of the people and institutions that are part of the CC movement are not formally connected to Creative Commons.

Creative Commons has a formal CC Global Network,[3] which includes lawyers, activists, scholars, artists, and more, all working on a wide range of projects and issues connected to sharing and collaboration. But the CC Global Network is just one player in the larger open movement, which includes Wikipedians, Mozillians, open access advocates, and many more.

Open source software is cited as the first domain where networked open sharing produced a tangible benefit as a movement that went much further than technology. The Conversation website's Explainer summarizes other movements (http://theconversation.com/explainer-what-is-the-open-movement-10308) adds other examples, such as Open Innovation in the corporate world, Open Data (see the Open Data Commons at https://opendatacommons.org), and Crowdsourcing. There is also the Open Access movement, which aims to make research widely available; the Open Science movement; and the growing movement around Open Educational Resources.

CREATIVE COMMONS: THE ORGANIZATION

Creative Commons is a small nonprofit organization that stewards the CC legal tools and helps power the open movement. Creative Commons is a distributed organization, with CC staff and contractors working around the world.

In 2016, Creative Commons embarked on a new organizational strategy based on building and sustaining a vibrant, usable commons, powered by collaboration and gratitude.[4] This is a shift from focusing only on the number of works out there under CC licenses and available for reuse, to a new emphasis on the connections and collaborations which happen around that content.

Guided by that strategy, Creative Commons' organizational work loosely falls into two main buckets:

- *Licenses, tools, and technology:* The CC licenses and public domain tools are the core legal tools designed and stewarded by Creative Commons. While our licenses have been rigorously vetted by legal experts around the globe, our work is still not done. We are actively working on technical infrastructure designed to make it easier to find and use all the content in the digital commons. We are also thinking about ways to better adapt all of Creative Commons' legal and technical tools for today's web.
- *Supporting the movement:* Creative Commons works to help people within open movements collaborate on projects and work toward similar goals. Through CC's multiple programs, we work directly with our global community—across education, culture, science, copyright reform, government policy, and other sectors—to help train and empower open advocates around the world.

Final Remarks

Creative Commons has grown from its home in a law school basement into a global organization with a wide reach and a well-known name associated with a core set of shared values. It is, at one and the same time, a set of licenses, a movement, and a nonprofit organization. We hope this chapter has helped give you a sense of what the organization does and, even more importantly, how you can join us in our work.

1.3 | ADDITIONAL RESOURCES

MORE INFORMATION ABOUT CC HISTORY

- "How I Lost the Big One," by Lawrence Lessig.
  Lawrence Lessig describes the details of the *Eldred* case: http://www .legalaffairs.org/issues/March-April-2004/story_lessig_marapr04.msp.

- Excerpt from Free Culture, by Lawrence Lessig. CC BY-NC 1.0.
  This is an excerpt that provides more background on the *Eldred vs. Ashcroft* case: http://www.authorama.com/free-culture-18.html.

MORE INFORMATION ABOUT CC AND OPEN LICENSING

- *Why Open Education Matters*, by David Blake @ Degreed. CC BY 3.0.
  This is a brief video that explains how open education is enabled by the Internet, why it is valuable for the global community, and how Creative Commons licenses enable open education: https://www.youtube.com/watch?v=gJWbVt2Nc-I.

- "We Copy like We Breathe," by Cory Doctorow.
  This is a keynote address that explains copying and how the Internet has changed the space of copying. It frames the need for adequate licensing as we copy and share online: https://www.youtube.com/watch?v=h-fU6e6--izo.

- "We Need to Talk about Sharing," by Ryan Merkley @ Creative Commons. CC BY-SA 3.0.
  This is a brief discussion about the value of sharing, how sharing can improve communities, and how Creative Commons enables sharing: https://vimeo.com/151666798.

MORE INFORMATION ABOUT THE COMMONS

- *How Does the Commons Work*, by the Next System Project, adapted from *Commoning as a Transformative Social Paradigm*. CC BY 3.0.
  This video, adapted from the economist David Bollier's explanation of what a commons is, explains how a commons works and describes threats to the commons: https://www.youtube.com/watch?v=7bQiB cd7mBc.

- "The Commons Short and Sweet," by David Bollier. CC BY 3.0.
  This is a brief blog post explanation of a commons, some problems of a commons, and what enables a commons to occur: http://bollier.org/commons-short-and-sweet.

- *The Wealth of the Commons: A World beyond Market and State*, by David Bollier and Silke Helfrich. CC BY-SA 3.0.
  This book seeks many voices to gather descriptions of what types of resources exist in the commons, the geographic circumstances relating

to the commons, and the political relevance of the commons: http://
wealthofthecommons.org.

- "Enclosure," *Wikipedia* article. CC BY-SA 3.0.
  This is an article describing enclosure, which is an issue that presents
  itself in a commons: https://en.wikipedia.org/wiki/Enclosure.

- "The Political Economy of the Commons," by Yochai Benkler. CC BY 3.0.
  This is a brief article that explains how a common infrastructure can
  sustain the commons: https://web.archive.org/web/20130617041302/
  http://www.boell.org/downloads/Benkler_The_Political_Economy_of
  _the_commons.pdf.

- "The Tragedy of the Commons," by Boundless and Lumen Learning.
  This is a section of an economics course textbook that explains the
  economic principles underlying potential threats to the commons:
  https://www.boundless.com/economics/textbooks/boundless
  -economics-textbook/market-failure-public-goods-and-common
  -resources-8/common-resources-62/the-tragedy-of-the-commons
  -235-12326.

- "Debunking the Tragedy of the Commons," by On the Commons. CC BY-SA
  3.0.
  This is a short article describing how the "tragedy" of the commons can
  be overcome: http://www.onthecommons.org/debunking-tragedy
  -commons.

- "Elinor Ostrom's 8 Principles for Managing a Commons," by On the
  Commons. CC BY-SA 3.0.
  This is a short history of the economist Elinor Ostrom and the eight
  principles that she has established for managing a commons: http://
  www.onthecommons.org/magazine/elinor-ostroms-8-principles
  -managing-commmons.

MORE INFORMATION ABOUT OTHER OPEN MOVEMENTS

- *Free Culture Game*, by Molle Industria. CC BY-NC-SA 3.0.
  This is a game to help understand the concept of free culture: http://
  www.molleindustria.org/en/freeculturegame.

Participants' Recommended Resources

CC Certificate participants have recommended many additional resources through Hypothes.is annotations on the Certificate website. While Creative Commons has not vetted these resources, we wanted to highlight the participants' contributions here: https://certificates.creativecommons.org/cccertedu comments/chapter/additional-resources.

NOTES

1. David Bollier, "The Commons, Short and Sweet," David Bollier (blog), July 15, 2011, http://www.bollier.org/commons-short-and-sweet. CC BY 3.0.

2. While other custom open copyright licenses have been developed in the past, we recommend using Creative Commons licenses because they are up-to-date, free to use, and have been broadly adopted by governments, institutions, and individuals as the global standard for open copyright licenses.

3. The work of the CC Global Network is organized into what we call "Network Platforms"; think of them as working groups. Anyone interested in working on a Platform can join and contribute as much or as little time and effort as they choose. Read more about our Network Platforms at https://creative commons.org/about/global-affiliate-network/network-platforms/ to see if there is an area of work that interests you. If interested, please get involved!

4. For more information on this policy, see https://creativecommons.org/use-remix/ ideas.

Copyright Law

CREATIVE COMMONS LICENSES DO NOT REPLACE COPYRIGHT. THEY ARE BUILT on top of it. The default of "all rights reserved" copyright means that all rights to copy and adapt a work are reserved by the author or creator (with some important exceptions that you will learn about shortly). By contrast, Creative Commons licenses adopt a "some rights reserved" approach, enabling authors or creators to free up their works for reuse by the public under certain conditions. To understand how Creative Commons licenses work, it is important that you have a basic understanding of copyright.

This chapter has five sections:

1. Copyright Basics
2. Global Aspects of Copyright
3. The Public Domain
4. Exceptions and Limitations of Copyright
5. Additional Resources

This chapter is important because Creative Commons licenses and public domain tools depend on copyright in order to work. While some aspects of copyright law have been harmonized around the world, the laws of copyright generally vary—sometimes dramatically—from country to country. The information contained in this chapter is not intended to be exhaustive or to cover all aspects of the complex laws of copyright around the world, or even every aspect of copyright that may impact how the CC licenses operate in a particular situation. It is intended to provide an overview of the basic concepts that are most important for an understanding of how Creative Commons licenses operate.

2.1 | COPYRIGHT BASICS

Is copyright confusing to you? Let's get some clarity by understanding its history and purpose.

THE BIG QUESTION: WHY IT MATTERS

Why do we have laws that restrict the copying and sharing of creative work? (Note: A "creative work" can be anything that is an original work. These can range from novels, poems, and plays to movies, TV shows, and videos; to songs and other musical compositions; to paintings, drawings, and sculptures; to all sorts of books, articles, and essays; computer programs; cartoons and comic books; and even the drawings our children make and our own jottings on a napkin. Anything we write, film, or record is a "creative work" as long as it is an original product and is fixed in a tangible form or medium.) And how do laws that restrict the copying of creative work function in the context of the Internet, where nearly everything we do involves making a copy?

Copyright law is an important area of law, one that reaches into nearly every facet of our lives, whether we know it or not. Aspects of our lives that in some instances are not regulated by copyright—like reading a physical book—become regulated by copyright when technology is used to share the same book by posting it to the Internet. Because almost everything we do online involves making a copy, copyright has become a regular feature in our lives.

LEARNING OUTCOMES
- Trace the basic history of copyright
- Explain the purpose of copyright
- Explain how copyright is automatic
- Explain general copyright terms

PERSONAL REFLECTION: WHY IT MATTERS TO YOU

Think back to a time when you invested significant effort in a creative project. What was your motivation for doing so? Did you know at the time that you were creating a work which is very likely protected by copyright, which restricts most reuses of that work by others without your permission? Did knowing that, or would knowing that, have made a difference to you? If so, why?

Acquiring Essential Knowledge

You might not realize it, but copyright law is as integral to your daily life as local traffic laws. Copyright law is the area of law that limits how others may use the original works of authors (or creators, as we often call them)—works spanning the spectrum from novels and operas, to cat videos, to scribbles on a napkin.

Although copyright laws vary from country to country, there are certain commonalities among these laws globally. This is largely due to international treaties. These treaties are explained in detail in section 2.2 "Global Aspects of Copyright."

There are some important fundamentals you need to be aware of regarding what is copyrightable, as well as who controls the rights and can grant permission to reuse a copyrighted work.

1. *Copyright grants a set of exclusive rights to creators*, which means that no one else can copy, distribute, perform, adapt, or otherwise use their work in violation of those exclusive rights. This gives creators the means to control the use of their works by others, thereby incentivizing them to create new works in the first place. The person who *controls the rights*, however, may not always be the author. It is important to understand who controls the exclusive rights granted by copyright in order to understand who has authority to grant permissions to others to reuse the work (e.g., by adding a CC license to the work). For example:

   - Work created in the course of your employment may be subject to differing degrees of employer ownership based on your jurisdiction. Australia, Japan, the United Kingdom, and the United States adhere to some form of a doctrine commonly known as "work for hire." This doctrine generally provides that if you have created a copyrightable work within the scope of your employment, the employer is the owner of, and controls the economic rights in the copyrighted work, even though you are the author and may retain your moral rights.
   - Independent contractors may or may not own and control copyright in the works they create in that capacity—this determination almost always depends on the terms of the contract between you and the organization that engaged you to perform the work, even though you are the author and may have moral rights.
   - Teachers, university faculty, and learners may or may not own and control copyright in the works they create in those capacities—that

determination will depend on certain laws (such as work for hire in some instances) and on the terms of the employment or contractor agreement, university or school policies, and terms of enrollment at the particular institution, even though they are the creators and may have moral rights.

- If you have co-created an original work that is subject to copyright, you may be a joint owner, not an exclusive owner, of the rights granted by copyright law. Joint ownership generally allows all owners to exercise the exclusive rights granted by law, but requires the owners to be accountable to one another for certain uses they make of their joint work.

- Ownership and control of the rights afforded by copyright laws are complicated. For more information, please see the "Additional Resources" section at the end of this chapter.

2. Copyright *does not protect facts or ideas* themselves, only the *expression* of those facts or ideas. This may sound simple, but unfortunately it is not. The difference between an *idea* and the *expression* of that idea can be tricky, but it's also extremely important to understand. While copyright law gives creators control over the expression of an idea, it does not allow the copyright holder to own or exclusively control the idea itself.

3. As a general rule, copyright is *automatic* the moment a work is fixed in a tangible medium. For example, you have a copyright as soon as you type the first stanza of your poem or record a song in most countries. Registering your copyright with a local copyright authority allows you to officially record your authorship, and in some countries this may be necessary to enforce your rights or might provide you with certain other advantages. But generally speaking, you do not have to register your work to become a copyright holder.

4. Copyright protection *lasts a long time.* We will say more about this later, but for now it's enough to know that copyright lasts a long time, often many decades after the creator dies.

> **NOTE** The combination of very long terms of copyright protection with automatic entry into the copyright system has created a massive amount of "orphan works"—copyrighted works for which the copyright holder is unknown or impossible to locate.

A SIMPLE HISTORY OF COPYRIGHT

Arguably, the world's most important early copyright law was enacted in 1710 in England: the Statute of Anne, "An act for the encouragement of learning, by vesting the copies of printed books in the authors or purchasers of such copies, during the times therein mentioned."[1] This law gave book publishers fourteen years of legal protection from the copying of their books by others.

Since then, the scope of the exclusive rights granted under copyright has expanded. Today, copyright law extends far beyond books to cover nearly anything with even a fragment of creativity or originality created by humans.

Additionally, the duration of the exclusive rights has also expanded. Today, in many parts of the world, the term of copyright granted an individual creator is the life of the creator plus an additional fifty years. See the "Worldwide Map of Copyright Term Length" (figure 2.3) in section 2.2 "Global Aspects of Copyright" (below) for more details about the duration of copyright and its variances worldwide.

And finally, since the Statute of Anne, copyright treaties have been signed by many countries. The result is that copyright laws have been harmonized to some degree around the world. You will learn more about the most important treaties and how copyright laws work around the world in section 2.2.

THE PURPOSE OF COPYRIGHT

There are two primary rationales for copyright law, though rationales do vary among legal traditions. The two rationales are:

- *Utilitarian:* Under this rationale, copyright is designed to provide an incentive to creators. The aim is to encourage the creation of new works.
- *Author's rights:* Under this rationale, copyright is primarily intended to ensure attribution for authors and preserve the integrity of creative works. The aim is to recognize and protect the deep connection that authors have with their creative works. (You can learn more about author's rights in the "Additional Resources" section at the end of this chapter.)

While different legal systems identify more strongly with one or the other of these rationales, or have other justifications particular to their legal traditions, many copyright systems are influenced by and draw from both rationales (due, in large part, to historical reasons that are outside the scope of this material).

Do one or both of these justifications resonate with you? What other reasons do you believe support or don't support the granting of exclusive rights to the creators of original works?

Drawing on the author's rights tradition, most countries also have *moral rights* that protect, sometimes indefinitely, the bond between authors and their creative output. Moral rights are distinct from the rights granted to copyright holders to restrict others from economically exploiting their works, but they are closely connected.

The two most common types of moral rights are the *right to be recognized as the author of the work* (known traditionally as the "right of paternity") and the *right to protect the work's integrity* (generally, the right to object to distortion of or the introduction of undesired changes to the work).

Not all countries have moral rights, but in some parts of the world they are considered so integral that they cannot be licensed away or waived by creators, and they last indefinitely.

HOW COPYRIGHT WORKS: A PRIMER

Copyright applies to works of original authorship, which means works that are unique and not a copy of someone else's work, and most of the time this requires the works' fixation in a tangible medium (written down, recorded, saved to your computer, etc.).

Copyright law establishes the basic terms of use that apply automatically to these original works. These terms give the creator or owner of copyright certain exclusive rights, while also recognizing that users have certain rights to use these works without the need for a license or permission.

What's copyrightable?

In countries that have signed on to the major copyright treaties described in more detail in section 2.2, copyright exists in the following general categories of works, though sometimes special rules apply on a country-by-country basis. A specific country's copyright laws almost always further specify different

Watch *Copy (aka copyright) Tells the Story of His Life* from #FixCopyright for a short history of copyright and its relation to creativity and sharing. **https://www.youtube.com/watch?v=ofdU DecJ6jc** | CC BY 3.0

types of works within each category. Can you think of a type of work within each category?

- Literary, artistic, musical, and dramatic works
- Translations, adaptations, arrangements, and alterations of literary, artistic, and musical works
- Collections of literary and artistic works[2]
- Additionally, depending on the country, original works of authorship may also include, among others:
  - » Applied art and industrial designs and models
  - » Computer software

What are the exclusive rights granted?

Creators who have copyright have exclusive rights to control certain uses of their works by others, such as the following (note that other rights may exist depending on the country):

- to make copies of their works
- to publicly perform and communicate their works to the public, including via broadcast
- to make adaptations and arrangements of their works (Adaptations can include translations.)

This means that if you own the copyright to a particular book, no one else can copy or adapt that book without your permission (with important caveats, which we will get to later in section 2.3 "Global Aspects of Copyright"). Keep in mind that there is an important difference between being the copyright holder of a novel and controlling how a particular authorized copy of the novel is used. While the copyright owner owns the exclusive rights to make copies of the novel, the person who owns a particular physical copy of that novel can generally do what they want with it, such as loan it to a friend or sell it to a used bookstore.

One of the exclusive rights of copyright is the right to adapt a work. An adaptation (or a "derivative work," as it is sometimes called) is a new work based on a preexisting work. In some countries, the term *derivative work* is used to describe changes that include but are not limited to "adaptations" as described in the Berne Convention for the Protection of Literary and Artistic Works, which uses both of these terms in different articles. For the purposes of this book and for understanding how CC licenses and public domain tools work, the terms *derivative work* and *adaptation* are interchangeable and denote a work that has been created from a preexisting work through changes that can only be made with the permission of the copyright holder. It is important to note that not all changes to an existing work require permission. Generally, a modification rises to the level of an adaptation or derivative when the modified work is based on the prior work and manifests sufficient new creativity to be copyrightable, such as a translation of a novel from one language to another, or the creation of a screenplay based on a novel.

Copyright owners often grant permission to others to adapt their work. Adaptations are entitled to their own copyright, but that protection only applies to the new elements that are particular to the adaptation. For example, if the author of a poem gives someone permission to make an adaptation, that person may rearrange stanzas, add new stanzas, and change some of the wording, among other things. Generally, the original author retains all copyright in the elements of the poem that remain in the adaptation, and the person adapting the poem has a copyright in their new contributions to the adapted poem. Creating a derivative work does not eliminate the copyright held by the creator of the preexisting work.

A special note about additional exclusive rights

There are two other categories of rights that are important to understand because the rights are licensed and referenced by Creative Commons licenses and public domain tools:

- *Moral rights:* As mentioned above, moral rights are an integral feature of many countries' copyright laws. These rights are recognized in Article *6bis* of the Berne Convention for the Protection of Literary and Artistic Works—described in more detail in section 2.2—and are integrated in the laws of all treaty signatories to some extent. Creative Commons licenses and legal tools account for these moral rights, and the reality is that they cannot be waived or licensed in many countries, even though other exclusive economic rights are waivable or licensable.
- *Similar and related rights* (including rights known in many countries as "neighboring rights"): Closely related to copyright are similar and related rights. These are rights that relate to copyrighted works and grant additional exclusive rights beyond the basic rights granted authors that were described above. Some of these rights are governed by international treaties, but they also vary country by country. Generally, these rights are

designed to give some "copyright-like" rights to those who are not them-selves the author but are involved in communicating the work to the public, for example, broadcasters and performers. Some countries like Japan have established these rights as part of copyright itself, while other countries treat these rights separately from, though closely related to, copyright.

> » The term *Similar Rights* is used to describe these similar and related rights in CC licenses and CC0, as you will learn in the next chapter in section 3.2.

> » An in-depth discussion of these rights is beyond the scope of this unit. What is important to be aware of is that they exist, and that Creative Commons licenses and public domain tools cover these rights, thereby allowing those who have such rights to use CC tools to give the public permission to use works in ways that would oth-erwise violate those rights.

Does the public have any right to use copyrighted works that do not violate the exclusive rights of creators?

All countries that have signed on to major international treaties grant the public some rights to use copyrighted works without permission, and without violat-ing the exclusive rights given creators. These are generally called "exceptions and limitations" to copyright. Many countries itemize the specific exceptions and limitations on which the public may rely, while some countries have flex-ible exceptions and limitations such as the concept of "fair use" in the United States, "fair dealing" in some Commonwealth countries, and education-spe-cific exceptions and limitations in many other parts of the world, including the Global South. Exploring these concepts in detail is reserved for section 2.4 "Exceptions and Limitations of Copyright." What is important to know is that copyright law does not require permission from the creator for every use of a copyrighted work—some uses are permitted as a matter of copyright policy, which balances the sometimes competing interests of the copyright owner and the public.

What else should I know about copyright?

As noted at the beginning of this chapter, copyright is complex and varies around the world. This chapter serves as a general introduction to its central concepts. There are some concepts, such as (1) liability and remedies, (2) licens-ing and transfer, and (3) termination of copyright transfers and licenses, that you should be aware of because you are likely to encounter them at some point. You will find a comprehensive explanation of these concepts in the "Additional Resources" section at the end of this chapter.

Distinguishing Copyright from Other Types of Intellectual Property

Intellectual property is the term used for rights—established by law—that empower creators to restrict others from using their creative works. Copyright is one type of intellectual property, but there are many others. To help understand copyright, it is important to have a basic understanding of at least two other types of intellectual property rights and the laws that protect those rights.

- *Trademark law* generally protects the public from being confused about the source of a good, service, or establishment. The holder of a trademark is generally allowed to prevent uses of its trademark by others if the public will be confused. Examples of trademarks are the golden arches used by McDonald's and the brand name Coca-Cola. Trademark law helps producers of goods and services protect their reputation, and it protects the public by giving them a simple way to differentiate between similar products and services.
- *Patent law* gives inventors a time-limited monopoly to their inventions— things like mousetraps or new mobile phone technology. Patents typically give inventors the exclusive right to make, have made, use, have used, offer for sale, sell, have sold, or import patentable inventions.

Other types of intellectual property rights include trade secrets, publicity rights, and moral rights, to give just a few examples.

Final Remarks

Digital technology has made it easier than ever to copy and reuse works that others have created, and it has made it easier than ever to create and share your own work. In short, copyright is everywhere. Since nearly every use of a work

For a brief introduction to the different types of intellectual property, watch the three-minute video *How to Register a Trademark (Canada): Trademarks, Patents and Copyrights – What's the Difference?* **https://www.youtube.com/watch?v=IVYAOy466vs** | CC BY 3.0

online involves making a copy, copyright law plays a role in nearly everything we do online.

2.2 | GLOBAL ASPECTS OF COPYRIGHT

Copyright laws vary from country to country, yet we operate in a world where media is global. Over time, there has been an effort to standardize copyright laws around the globe.

FIGURE 2.1 **"MG_0033"**
Photo from Flickr: flickr.com/photos/48656755@N00/4188202128
Author: pedist | CC BY 2.0 | Desaturated from original

LEARNING OUTCOMES
- Learn how the copyright laws of your country may differ from those of other countries
- Identify major international treaties and efforts to harmonize copyright laws around the world

THE BIG QUESTION: WHY IT MATTERS
Although copyright laws differ from country to country, the Internet has made global distribution and sharing of copyrightable works possible with just the click of a button. What does this mean for you, when you share your works on the Internet and use works published by others outside your country? What

law applies to a video taken by someone from India during their travels in Kenya and then posted to YouTube? What about when that video is watched or downloaded by someone in Canada?

Copyright law is locally implemented by every country around the world. In an effort to minimize complexity, efforts have been undertaken to harmonize some of the basic elements of how copyright works across the globe.

PERSONAL REFLECTION: WHY IT MATTERS TO YOU
When you publish or reuse something online, have you ever thought about what law applies to you? Does it make sense to you that different people should have different limits to what they can do with your work based on their geographic location? Why or why not?

Acquiring Essential Knowledge: Introduction to the Global Copyright System

INTERNATIONAL LAWS
Every country has its own copyright laws, but over the years there has been extensive global harmonization of copyright laws through treaties and multilateral and bilateral trade agreements. These treaties and agreements establish minimum standards for all participating countries, which then enact or amend their own laws in order to conform to the agreed-upon limits. This system leaves room for local variations.

These treaties and agreements are negotiated in various forums: the World Intellectual Property Organization (WIPO), the World Trade Organization (WTO), and in private negotiations between countries.

One of the most significant international agreements on copyright law is the Berne Convention for the Protection of Literary and Artistic Works (the "Berne Convention"), concluded in 1886. The Berne Convention has since been revised and amended on several occasions. WIPO serves as the administrator of the treaty and its revisions and amendments, and is the depository for official instruments of accession to and ratification of the treaty. Today, 177 countries (as of October 17, 2019) have signed the Berne Convention. This treaty (as amended and revised) lays out several fundamental principles upon which all the participating countries have agreed. One of these principles is that copyright must be granted automatically—that is, there must be *no legal formalities* required to obtain copyright protection (for example, the national laws of the signatories cannot require you to register or pay for your copyright as a con-

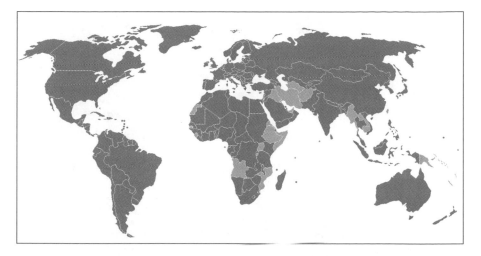

FIGURE 2.2 **World map showing the parties to the Berne convention, 2012**

The signatories of the Berne Convention for the Protection of Literary and Artistic Works, as of 2012

Figure from Wikimedia Commons: https://commons .wikimedia.org/wiki/File:Berne_Convention.png CC BY-SA 3.0 | Desaturated from original

dition for receiving copyright protection). In general, the Berne Convention as revised and amended also requires that all countries give foreign works the same protection they give to works created within their borders, assuming the other country is a signatory. Figure 2.2 is a map showing (in dark gray) the signatories to the Berne Convention as of 2012.

Additionally, the Berne Convention sets minimum standards—default rules—for the duration of copyright protection for creative works, though some exceptions exist, depending on the subject matter. The Berne Convention's standards for copyright protection dictate a minimum term of the life of the author plus 50 years. Because the Berne Convention sets minimums only, several countries have established *longer* terms of copyright for individual creators, such as "life of the author plus 70 years" or "life of the author plus 100 years." You can review the *Wikipedia* article on "Copyright Term" (licensed CC BY-SA 3.0, available at https://en.wikipedia.org/ wiki/Copyright_term) and view the page that lists the duration of copyright based on country (also licensed CC BY-SA 3.0, available at https://en.wiki pedia.org/wiki/List_of_countries%27_copyright_lengths). The map in figure 2.3 shows the status of copyright duration around the world as of 2012.

In addition to the Berne Convention, several other international agreements have further harmonized copyright rules around the world.[3]

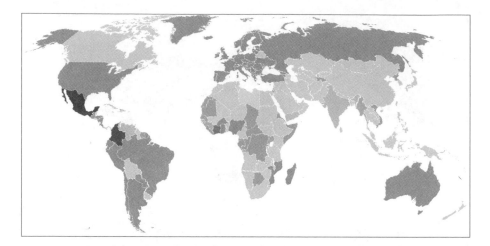

FIGURE 2.3 **Worldwide map of copyright term length**

Figure from Wikimedia Commons: https://commons
.wikimedia.org/wiki/File:World_copyright_terms.svg
Author: Balfour Smith, Canuckguy, Badseed, Martsniez
Original image by Balfour Smith at Duke University
CC BY 3.0 | Desaturated from original

NATIONAL LAWS

Although an international framework exists because of the Berne Convention and other treaties and agreements, copyright law is actually enacted and enforced through national laws. Those laws are supported by national copyright offices, which in turn support copyright holders, allow for registration, and provide interpretative guidance. As mentioned, while there has been a major effort to create minimum standards for copyright across the globe, countries still have a significant amount of discretion as to how they meet the requirements imposed by the various treaties and agreements. This means that the details of copyright law still vary quite a bit from country to country.

Which nation's law applies to my use of a work restricted by copyright?

A common question of copyright creators and users of their works is which nation's copyright law applies to a particular use of a particular work. Generally, the rule of territoriality applies: national laws are limited in their reach to activities taking place within that country. This also means that generally speaking, the law of the country *where a work is used* applies to that particular use. If you are distributing a book in a particular country, then the law of the country where you are distributing the book generally applies.

This is true even in the era of the Internet, though it is much harder to apply. For example, if you are a Canadian citizen traveling to Germany and using a copyrighted work in your PowerPoint presentation, then German copyright law normally applies to your use.

It can be complicated to determine which national law applies in any given case. This complexity is one of the benefits of Creative Commons licenses, which are designed to be enforceable everywhere.

Final Remarks

Even though global copyright treaties and agreements exist, there is no one "international copyright law." Different countries have different standards for what is protected by copyright, how long copyright lasts and what it restricts, and what penalties apply when it is infringed.

2.3 | THE PUBLIC DOMAIN

The "public domain" consists of creative works that are not subject to copyright. This is the enormous pool of publicly available material which circulates freely, and from which new creative works and knowledge may be built. Figure 2.4 shows a still from the 1902 French film *Le Voyage dans la lune* (*A Trip to the Moon*), which is now in the public domain.

FIGURE 2.4
A still from the 1902 film
Le Voyage dans la Lune
(*A Trip to the Moon*)

Image from Wikimedia Commons:
*https://commons.wikimedia.org/
wiki/File:Melies_color_Voyage
_dans_la_lune.jpg*
Author: Georges Méliès
A work in the public domain

LEARNING OUTCOMES
- Explain what the public domain is
- Communicate the value of the public domain

THE BIG QUESTION: WHY IT MATTERS

Why is it important that works eventually fall out of copyright? Are there any works that do not qualify for copyright protection and may be freely used?

A critical aspect of copyright law is that the protection it provides does not last forever. After a set term, the copyright expires and the work enters the public domain for everyone to copy, adapt, and share. Likewise, there are certain types of works that fall outside the scope of copyright.

PERSONAL REFLECTION: WHY IT MATTERS TO YOU

Have you ever seen ancient Egyptian sculptures in real life? Have you ever listened to a Beethoven symphony? Have you ever read Tolstoy's novel *War and Peace*? These works are in the public domain. What other public domain works have you enjoyed in your lifetime? Have you ever created something new using a work in the public domain?

Acquiring Essential Knowledge

Despite the expansive reach of copyright, there is still a rich (and growing) public domain full of works which are free from copyright. Works enter the public domain in one of four ways:

1. *The copyright expires.*

   While copyright terms are longer than ever before, they are not infinite. In most countries, the term of an individual's copyright expires 50 years after her death. In some countries, the term is longer and can be up to 100 years after the author dies. Review the map in figure 2.3 (earlier in this chapter) for an overview of copyright terms around the world.

2. *The work was never entitled to copyright protection.*

   Copyright covers vast amounts of content created by authors, but certain categories of works fall outside the scope of copyright. For example, works that are purely functional are not copyrightable, like the design of a screw. The Berne Convention identifies additional categories that

> **NOTE** Moral rights may continue to exist in works that have otherwise entered the public domain. See section 2.1 "Copyright Basics."

FIGURE 2.5 **Creative Commons CC0 Icon**

The CC icons are visual symbols that convey the basic permissions associated with a particular type of CC license or tool.

Available for download at https:// creativecommons.org/about/downloads

cannot be copyrighted, such as official texts of a legislative, administrative, and legal nature. Furthermore, in some countries, works created by government employees are excluded from copyright protection and are not eligible for copyright. Facts and ideas are never copyrightable.

3. *The creator dedicates the work to the public domain before its copyright has expired.*

   In most parts of the world, a creator can decide to forego the protections of copyright and dedicate their work to the public domain. Creative Commons has a legal tool called CC0 ("CC Zero") Public Domain Dedication that helps authors put their works into the worldwide public domain to the greatest extent possible. You'll learn more about this tool (and other Creative Commons legal tools) later in this book.

4. *The copyright holder failed to comply with the formalities required to acquire or maintain their copyright.*

   Today in most countries, there are no formal requirements to acquire or renew copyright protection over a work. This was not always the case, however, and many works have entered the public domain over the years because a creator failed to adhere to these formalities.

WHAT CAN YOU DO WITH A WORK THAT IS IN THE PUBLIC DOMAIN?

You can do almost anything, but it depends on the scope and duration of copyright protection in the particular country where the work is used. Depending on the country, for example, a work in the public domain may still be covered by moral rights that last beyond the duration of copyright. It's also possible that a work is in the public domain in one country but is still under copyright in another country. This means you may not be able to use the work freely where copyright still applies.

AUTHOR CREDIT AND THE PUBLIC DOMAIN

Even though it may not be legally required in every country, and especially in those countries where moral rights do not exist after the term of copyright expires, there are many benefits to identifying and giving credit to the original creators, even after their work has entered the public domain. Many communities have adopted norms, which are accepted standards for crediting the authors and the treatment of works in the public domain. Creative Commons has created public domain guidelines that can be used by communities to create their own norms. You can review the CC guidelines at https://wiki.creativecommons.org/wiki/Public_Domain_Guidelines. Can you think of a reason why it might be helpful to give credit to an author whose work is in the public domain? Can you think of why norms should be encouraged when public domain works are reused?

FINDING WORKS IN THE PUBLIC DOMAIN

With millions of creative works whose copyright has expired—and many more added regularly with tools like the CC0 Public Domain Dedication—the public domain is a vast treasure trove of content.

Among the sites that host works in the public domain are Project Gutenberg, Public Domain Review, Digital Public Library of America, Wikimedia Commons, Internet Archive, Library of Congress, Flickr, and the Rijksmuseum. The CC Search tool (https://search.creativecommons.org/) is another way to find public domain material.

It is not always easy to identify whether a work is in the public domain (though there are many resources available to help). As we learned, copyright protection is automatic, so the absence of the copyright symbol "©" does not mean a work is in the public domain. In addition to its CC0 Public Domain Dedication for creators, Creative Commons also has a tool called the Public

NOTE A work that is in the public domain for purposes of copyright law may still be subject to other intellectual property restrictions. For example, a story that is in the public domain may have a trademarked brand on the cover associated with the publisher of the book. Trademark protection is independent of copyright protection and may still exist even though the work is in the public domain as a matter of copyright. Also, once a creator uses a public domain work to turn it into a new work, the creator will have copyright on the portions of their new work that are original to them. As an example, the creator of a film adaptation based on a novel in the public domain will have copyright protection over the film, but not the underlying novel.

Domain Mark (https://creativecommons.org/share-your-work/public-domain/pdm), which is designed to label works whose copyright has expired everywhere in the world, so that reusers can easily identify those works as being in the worldwide public domain. As of 2016, CC's public domain tools were used on more than 90 million works.

Final Remarks

A healthy public domain is crucial to preserving our cultural heritage, inspiring new generations of creators, and increasing human knowledge. Because the scope and duration of copyright have grown so much over the years, it can be easy to forget that the public domain exists at all. But the public domain is a critical part of the bargain of copyright and works in the public domain are incredible resources that belong to all of us.

2.4 | EXCEPTIONS AND LIMITATIONS TO COPYRIGHT

The limitations and exceptions built into copyright, including "fair use" and "fair dealing" in some parts of the world, were designed to ensure that the rights of the public were not unduly restricted by copyright.

THE BIG QUESTION: WHY IT MATTERS

What would the world look like if copyright had no limits to what it prevented you from doing with copyrighted works?

Imagine resorting to Google's search engine on your laptop or smartphone to settle a disagreement with a friend about some bit of trivia. You type in your search query, and Google comes up empty. You then learn that a court has required Google to delete its entire web index because it never entered into copyright agreements with each individual author of each individual page on the web. By indexing a web page and showing the public a snippet of the contents in their search results, the court has declared that Google violates the copyrights of hundreds of millions of people and can no longer show those search results.

Fortunately, thanks to the exceptions and limitations built into copyright laws in much of the world, including the fair use doctrine under U.S. copyright law, this hypothetical scenario is unlikely to become reality in most countries. This is one of many illustrations that show why it is so important that copyright has built-in limitations and exceptions.

- State what limitations and exceptions to copyright are and why they exist
- Name a few common exceptions and limitations to copyright

PERSONAL REFLECTION: WHY IT MATTERS TO YOU
Have you ever made a copy of a creative work? Can you recall a time when you were studying and you included properly cited quotations in a research paper you wrote? Can you think of a way an exception or limitation to copyright has benefited you?

Acquiring Essential Knowledge
Copyright is not absolute. There are some uses of copyrighted works that do not require permission. These uses are limitations on the exclusive rights normally granted to copyright holders and are known as "exceptions and limitations" to copyright.

Fair use, fair dealing, and other exceptions and limitations to copyright are an extremely important part of copyright design. Some countries afford exceptions and limitations to copyright, such as fair dealing, while other countries do not offer them at all.[4] If your use of another person's copyrighted work is "fair use" or falls within another exception or limitation to copyright, then you are not infringing that creator's copyright.

When legislators created copyright protections, they realized that allowing copyright to restrict all the possible uses of creative works could be highly problematic. For example, how could scholars and critics write about plays, books, movies, or other artworks without quoting from them? (It would be extremely difficult.) And would copyright holders be inclined to provide licenses or other permission to people whose reviews of their works might be negative? (Probably not.)

For this and a range of other reasons, certain uses are explicitly carved out from copyright to widely different degrees depending on the jurisdiction— including *uses for the purposes of criticism, commentary, news reporting, teaching, scholarship, research, parody, and access for the visually impaired.* The use of copyrighted works—or portions of those works—for these purposes is not an infringement of those works' copyright when an exception or limitation to copyright applies. These uses are known as "fair use" or "fair dealing" in some parts of the world.

The Berne Convention first established the concept of "fair use" by providing the following in Article 9, section 2. This is known as the "three-step" test, and has been adopted in some form in several other treaties:

> It shall be a matter for legislation in the countries of the Union to permit the reproduction of such works in certain *special cases, provided that such reproduction does not conflict with a normal exploitation of the work and does not unreasonably prejudice the legitimate interests of the author.* (emphasis added)

For more information about the scope and use of the three-step test, read the short primer published by the Electronic Frontier Foundation at https://www.eff.org/files/filenode/three-step_test_fnl.pdf.

The exceptions and limitations to copyright vary by country. There are global discussions around how to harmonize them. A World Intellectual Property Organization study (https://www.wipo.int/edocs/mdocs/copyright/en/sccr_30/sccr_30_3.pdf) by Kenneth Crews compares the copyright exceptions and limitations for libraries in many countries around the world.

Generally speaking, there are two main ways in which limitations and exceptions are written into copyright law. The first is by listing specific activities that are excluded from the reach of copyright. For example, Japanese copyright law has a specific exemption allowing classroom broadcasts of copyrighted material. This approach has the benefit of providing clarity about precisely what uses by the public are allowed and are not considered infringing. However, it can also be limiting because anything not specifically on the list of exceptions may be deemed restricted by copyright.

The other approach is to include flexible guidelines about what is allowed in the spirit of the three-step test described above. Courts then determine exactly what uses are allowed without the permission of the copyright holder. The downside to flexible guidelines is that they leave more room for uncertainty. This is the approach used in the United States with fair use, although U.S. copyright law also has some specific exceptions to copyright written into the law as well. In the United States, fair use is determined using a four-factor test,[5] in which a federal court judge considers (1) the purpose and character of use, (2) the nature of the copyrighted work, (3) the amount and substantiality of the portion taken from the work, and (4) the effect of the use upon the potential market for the copyrighted work. (See the "Additional Resources" section at the end of this chapter for a good selection of publications that discuss fair use and other exceptions and limitations to copyright.)

Most countries also have compulsory licensing schemes, which are another form of limitation on the exclusive rights of copyright holders. These statutory systems make copyrighted content (for example, music) available for particular types of reuse without asking permission, but they require payment of specified (and non-negotiable) fees to the copyright owners. Compulsory licensing schemes permit anyone to make certain uses of copyrighted works so long as they pay a fee to the rights holder whose work will be used.

As an organization and a movement, Creative Commons supports strong exceptions and limitations to copyright. But the vision of Creative Commons—universal access to research and education and full participation in culture—will not be realized through licensing alone. Creative Commons supports a copyright system that appropriately balances the rights of creators and the rights of users and the general public.

Final Remarks

Like the public domain, the exceptions and limitations to copyright are just as important as the exclusive rights that copyright grants. Think of them as a safety valve for the public in order to be able to utilize copyrighted works for particular uses in the public interest. You should educate yourself about the exceptions and limitations that apply in your country, so you can take advantage of and advocate for these critical user rights.

2.5 | ADDITIONAL RESOURCES

More Information about Copyright Concepts

LIABILITY AND REMEDIES

Generally, to establish a claim of copyright infringement, a creator or holder of copyright need only show that they have a valid copyright in the work and that the defendant copied protected expression from the work. However, the intention of the alleged infringer may be relevant in some cases, such as if the defendant asserts that an exception or limitation applied to their use or that their work was independently created.

The copyright laws of some countries grant copyright holders statutory remedies for infringement. The type and amounts of remedies, including damages, are established by law. You should be aware of the existence of statutory damages and other remedies permitted by applicable law, including statutory provisions that award legal fees in some circumstances.

LICENSING AND TRANSFER
Many creators and copyright holders need help to fully exercise their exclusive rights or simply give others permission to exercise the rights granted by copyright law. Several options exist to do this. Some creators choose to license some or all of their rights, either exclusively or nonexclusively. Others choose to sell their rights outright and allow others to exercise them in their place, sometimes in exchange for royalty payments. There are often formalities associated with the sale or licensing of copyrights, including when a copyright license must be in writing, depending on the copyright law that applies.

TERMINATION OF COPYRIGHT TRANSFERS AND LICENSES
The laws of some countries grant copyright holders the right to terminate transfer agreements or licenses even if the transfer agreement or license doesn't allow it. In the United States, for example, copyright law provides two mechanisms for doing so, depending on when the transfer agreement or license became effective. For more information on these rights and a tool that allows creators and copyright holders to figure out if they have those rights, see https://rightsback.org.

OTHER GENERAL RESOURCES ON COPYRIGHT
- "CopyrightX," by Harvard Law School.
  This is a course on copyright provided by the Harvard Law School's HarvardX distance learning initiative: http://copyx.org/; http:// online-learning.harvard.edu/course/copyrightx.

- U.S. Copyright Office, Circular no. 1, "Copyright Basics": https://www.copy right.gov/circs/circ01.pdf.

- "Copyright for Educators & Librarians," by Coursera. All rights reserved.
  This is a course on copyright provided by Coursera: https://www .coursera.org/learn/copyright-for-education.

MORE ON PHILOSOPHIES OF COPYRIGHT
- "Philosophy of Copyright," *Wikipedia* article: https://en.wikipedia.org/ wiki/Philosophy_of_copyright. CC BY-SA 3.0.

- "Author's Rights," CC BY-SA 3.0. *Wikipedia* article: https://en.wikipedia .org/wiki/Authors%27_rights.

More Information about Limitations and Exceptions to Copyright

- Fair Use Evaluator
  This is an online tool to help users understand how to determine the "fairness" of use under U.S. copyright law, and work with materials under fair use: http://librarycopyright.net/resources/fairuse/index .php.

- Program on Information Justice and Intellectual Property, by American University Washington College of Law. CC BY 3.0.
  See this program's "Publications on Fair Use" to understand the underlying principles and best practices of fair use: http://pijip-impact.org/ fairuse/publications.

- "Copyright and Exceptions," by Kennisland. Marked with CC0 1.0 Public Domain Designation.
  This is an interactive map of European copyright exceptions: http:// copyrightexceptions.eu.

- *A Fair(y) Use Tale,* by Eric Faden. CC BY-NC-SA 3.0.
  This is a creative educational fair-use mashup which ironically makes use of clips from Disney films as it explains how copyright works. The discussion of fair use begins around the 6-minute 30-second mark in the video: https://cyberlaw.stanford.edu/blog/2007/03/fairy-use-tale.

More Information about the Public Domain

- "Copyright Term and the Public Domain in the United States," by the Cornell University Library's Copyright Information Center. CC BY 3.0.
  This provides copyright information on when resources fall into the public domain, depending on the circumstances under which they were written: http://copyright.cornell.edu/resources/publicdomain.cfm.

- Out of Copyright: Determining the Copyright Status of Works.
  This is a website to help determine the copyright status of a work and whether it has fallen into the public domain: http://outofcopyright.eu/.

- The Public Domain Manifesto, by Communia. GNU General Public License.
  This is a website with information about the public domain, the values

of some of its supporters, and some recommendations on how to use the public domain: http://publicdomainmanifesto.org/manifesto.html.

- Center for the Study of Public Domain, by Duke Law School.
  This website contains information and events regarding the public domain: https://law.duke.edu/cspd/.

- *Bound by Law? Tales from the Public Domain*, by Keith Aoki, James Boyle, and Jennifer Jenkins. CC BY-NC-SA 2.5.
  This is a comic book about intellectual property law and the public domain: https://law.duke.edu/cspd/comics/digital/.

- *Public Domain Review.*
  This is an online journal and not-for-profit project that showcases works which have entered the public domain. The journal is dedicated to the exploration of curious and compelling works from the history of art, literature, and ideas: https://publicdomainreview.org/.

- "It's Time to Protect the Public Domain," by Wikimedia Foundation. CC BY 3.0.
  This blog post provides information on some of the important details of the public domain, its legal backing, and the public interest: https://blog.wikimedia.org/2017/06/30/time-to-protect-pd/.

Participants' Recommended Resources

CC Certificate participants have recommended many additional resources through Hypothes.is annotations on the Certificate website. While Creative Commons has not vetted these resources, we want to highlight these participants' suggestions here: https://certificates.creativecommons.org/cccertedu comments/chapter/additional-resources-2.

NOTES

1. The Statute of Anne; April 10, 1710, 8 Anne, c. 19, Yale, The Avalon Project, https://avalon.law.yale.edu/18th_century/anne_1710.asp. All rights reserved.

2. By collections, we mean the assembly of separate and independent creative works into a collective whole. See chapter 4 for more discussion about collections.

3. These international agreements include the Agreement on Trade-Related Aspects of Intellectual Property Rights (TRIPS), negotiated by members of the World Trade Organization in 1994; and the WIPO Copyright Treaty (WCT), negotiated by members of the World Intellectual Property Organization in 1996. These agreements address similar issues and also new IP-related issues not covered

by the Berne Convention. Another manner in which copyright policy is made is through bilateral and multilateral trade agreements. As of 2017, there were several negotiations underway. These include the Regional Comprehensive Economic Partnership (RCEP) and the renegotiation of the North American Free Trade Agreement (NAFTA). A major drawback of multilateral trade negotiations is that they are typically conducted in secret with little or no participation from civil society organizations and the public.

4. The fair use doctrine is found in the United States, and the fair dealing doctrine is found in many other countries with common-law systems. You can learn more about the limitations and exceptions at https://www.wipo.int/copyright/en/limitations/ and https://en.wikipedia.org/wiki/Limitations_and_exceptions_to_copyright.

5. For more information on the four-factor test, see "Measuring Fair Use: The Four Factors," Stanford University Libraries, http://fairuse.stanford.edu/overview/fair-use/four-factors/.

Anatomy of a CC License

CREATIVE COMMONS LICENSES GIVE EVERYONE FROM INDIVIDUAL CREATORS to large companies and institutions a clear, standardized way to grant permission to others to use their creative work. From the reuser's perspective, the presence of a Creative Commons license answers the question, "What can I do with this?" and provides the freedom to reuse the work of others, subject to clearly defined conditions.

All CC licenses ensure that creators retain their copyright and get credit for their work, while still permitting others to copy and distribute it. Although the CC legal tools are designed to be as easy to use as possible, there are still some things to learn in order to fully understand their mechanics.

This chapter has five sections:

1. License Design and Terminology
2. License Scope
3. License Types
4. License Enforceability
5. Additional Resources

3.1 | LICENSE DESIGN AND TERMINOLOGY

Do you "speak CC" yet? This section covers the acronyms, terms, and icons used in connection with Creative Commons' tools, as well as some key things to know about how the licenses were designed.

LEARNING OUTCOMES
- Differentiate the meaning of different CC icons
- Identify the three layers of CC licenses

THE BIG QUESTION: WHY IT MATTERS
Given that most of us are not lawyers, what do we need to know about the legalities in order to use CC licenses properly?

Creative Commons' legal tools were designed to be as accessible to everyone as possible while still being legally robust. CC's founders made several design decisions that make these legal tools relatively easy to use and understand.

PERSONAL REFLECTION: WHY IT MATTERS TO YOU
Have you ever come across a CC-licensed Flickr image that you really liked but were afraid to use because you weren't sure of the legal terms and conditions? Have you ever been frustrated because you didn't understand how to decide which of the CC legal tools to use for your own work?

Acquiring Essential Knowledge

Copyright operates by default under an "all rights reserved" approach. Creative Commons licenses function within copyright law, but they utilize a "some rights reserved" approach. While there are several different CC license options, all of them grant permission to use the works under certain standardized conditions. The licenses grant those permissions for as long as the underlying copyright lasts or until/unless you violate the license terms. This is what we mean when we say CC licenses work on top of copyright, not instead of copyright.

The CC licenses were designed to be a free, voluntary solution for creators who want to grant the public up-front permission to use their works. Although the licenses are legally enforceable tools, they were designed in a way that was intended to make them accessible to non-lawyers.

The licenses are built using a three-layer design (figure 3.1).

1. The *legal code* is the base layer. This contains the "lawyer-readable" terms and conditions that are legally enforceable in court. Take a minute and scan through the legal code of CC BY (https://creativecommons.org/licenses/by/4.0/legalcode) to see how it is structured. Can you find where the attribution requirements are listed?
2. The *commons deeds* are the best-known layer of the licenses. These are the web pages that lay out the key license terms in "human-read-

able" terms. The deeds are not legally enforceable but instead summarize the legal code. Take some time to explore the deeds for CC BY (https://creative commons.org/licenses/by/4.0) and CC BY-NC-ND (https://creativecommons .org/licenses/by-nc-nd/4.0/) and identify how they differ. Can you find the links to the legal code from each deed?

3. The final layer of the license design recognizes that software plays a critical role in the creation, copying, discovery, and distribution of works. In order to make it easy for websites and web services to know when a work

FIGURE 3.1 **The three layers of a CC license**

is available under a Creative Commons license, we provide a "machine-readable" version of the license (see figure 3.2)—this is a summary of the key freedoms granted and obligations imposed, and is written into a format that applications, search engines, and other kinds of technology can understand. We developed a standardized way to describe licenses that software can understand called CC Rights Expression Language (CC REL) to accomplish this. When this metadata is attached to CC-licensed works, someone searching for a CC-licensed work using a search engine (e.g., Google Advanced Search) can more easily discover CC-licensed works.

FIGURE 3.2 **Example of "machine readable" code**

From Creative Commons License Chooser: https://creativecommons.org/ choose/
CC BY 4.0

CC LICENSE BASICS

All Creative Commons licenses have many important features in common. At a minimum, every license helps creators (we call them "licensors" when they use CC tools) retain copyright while allowing others to copy and distribute their work. Every CC license also ensures that licensors get credit for their work. CC licenses work around the world and last as long as the applicable copyright lasts (because they are built on copyright) and as long as the user complies with the license. These common features serve as the baseline, on top of which licensors can choose to grant additional permissions when deciding how they want their work to be used.

NOTE Throughout all of the CC Certificate content, please assume that all descriptions of the licenses refer to the most recent version of the CC license suite, Version 4.0, unless otherwise indicated. You will learn more about the different versions in section 3.3 "License Types."

CHOICES FOR THE LICENSOR

All Creative Commons licenses are structured to give the user permission to make a wide range of uses as long as the user complies with the conditions in the license. The basic condition in all of the licenses is that the user provides credit to the licensor and certain other information, such as where the original work may be found.

A CC licensor makes a few simple decisions on the path to choosing a license: first, do I want to allow commercial use of my work; and second, do I want to allow derivative works (also known as adaptations)? We'll address adaptations in greater detail within chapter 4.

If a licensor decides to allow derivative works, they may also choose to require that anyone who uses the work—we call them "licensees"—make their new work available under the same license terms. This is what is meant by "ShareAlike," and it is one of the mechanisms that has helped the digital commons of CC-licensed content grow over time. ShareAlike is inspired by the GNU General Public License, which is used by many free and open-source software projects.

These different license elements are symbolized by visual icons, as shown in figures 3.3a to 3.3d below.

The symbol shown in figure 3.3a means *Attribution* or "BY." This license means that others who use your work must give you credit for it (i.e., attribute it to you) in the way you request. All of the licenses include this condition.

FIGURES 3.3 A-D
Different license elements

The symbol shown in figure 3.3b means *NonCommercial* or "NC," which means the work is only available to be used for non-commercial purposes. Three of the CC licenses include this restriction.

The symbol shown in figure 3.3c means *ShareAlike* or "SA," which means that any adaptations and modified versions based on this work must adhere to the terms of the original license. Two of the CC licenses include this condition: Attribution-ShareAlike (CC BY-SA), and Attribution-NonCommercial-ShareAlike (CC BY-NC-SA).

The symbol shown in figure 3.3d means *NoDerivatives* or "ND," which means that reusers cannot share adaptations or modified versions of the work. Two of the CC licenses include this restriction: Attribution-NoDerivs (CC BY-ND), and Attribution-NonCommercial-NoDerivs (CC BY-NC-ND).

When combined, these icons represent the six CC license options. The icons are also embedded in the "license icons," which each represent a particular CC license type. The next section in this chapter, "License Types," explores the six combinations in detail.

FIGURE 3.4A **CC0**
FIGURE 3.4B **Public Domain Mark**

PUBLIC DOMAIN TOOLS

In addition to the CC license suite, Creative Commons also has two public domain tools, which are represented by the icons in figures 3.4a and 3.4b above. These public domain tools are not licenses.

CC0 (figure 3.4a) enables creators to dedicate their works to the worldwide public domain to the greatest extent possible. Note that some jurisdictions do not allow creators to dedicate their works to the public domain, so CC0 has other legal mechanisms included to help deal with this situation where it applies. (There is more on this in section 3.3 "License Types.")

The Public Domain Mark (figure 3.4b) is a label used to mark works that are known to be free of all copyright restrictions. Unlike CC0, the Public Domain Mark is *not* a legal tool and has no legal effect when applied to a work. It serves only as a label to inform the public about the public domain status of a work and is often used by museums and archives working with very old works.

Final Remarks

There is a learning curve to some of the terminology and basics about how CC legal tools work. But as you now know, it is far less intimidating than it looks. Now that you understand how to "speak CC" and know some of the fundamentals about CC license design, you are well on your way to becoming versed in CC licensing.

3.2 | LICENSE SCOPE

Creative Commons licenses are built on copyright law. This simple fact tells you most of what you need to know about when they do and do not apply, and how long they last.

LEARNING OUTCOMES
- Describe how CC works with copyright and why this is important
- Explain the time length of a CC license

THE BIG QUESTION: WHY IT MATTERS

What is the legal foundation upon which CC licenses operate? And why is this so important?

CC licenses are copyright licenses. They apply where and when copyright applies. This reflects a fundamental design decision by the founders of Creative Commons. Given that the goal was to make more creative and educational works available under common-sense terms, Creative Commons wanted to ensure that its licenses were not used to restrict works or uses of works that the copyright law does not restrict. This is a core CC value. Having the language of the licenses track copyright law accomplished this goal.

PERSONAL REFLECTION: WHY IT MATTERS TO YOU

Think about what it would mean if a CC license could prevent you from doing something you could otherwise do with a copyrighted work, such as printing a copy of a poem to insert in a birthday card for a friend. Do you understand why having CC licenses track copyright was an important decision for the founders of Creative Commons?

Acquiring Essential Knowledge

The statement that "Creative Commons licenses are copyright licenses" tells you the following about the licenses:

1. The licenses "operate" or apply only when the work is within the scope of copyright law (or other related laws) and the restrictions of copyright law apply to the intended use of the work. (This is discussed in more detail below.)
2. Certain other rights, such as patents, trademarks, and privacy and publicity rights are not covered by the licenses and must be managed separately.

The first of these statements explains a basic limitation of the licenses in controlling what people do with the work, and the second statement provides a warning that there may be other rights at play with the work that restrict how it is used.

WHAT DOES IT MEAN FOR THE CC LICENSE TO APPLY WHERE COPYRIGHT APPLIES?

CC licenses are appropriate for creators who have created something protectable by copyright, such as an image, an article, or a book, and who want to provide people with one or more of the permissions governed by copyright law. For example, if you want to give others permission to freely copy and redistribute your work, you can use a CC license to grant those permissions. Likewise, if you want to give others permission to freely transform, alter, or otherwise create derivative works based on your work, you can use a CC license to grant those permissions.

However, you don't need to use a Creative Commons license to give someone permission to read your article or watch your video, because reading and watching aren't activities that copyright generally regulates.

Here are two more important scenarios in which a user does not need a copyright license:[1]

- When fair use, fair dealing, or some other limitation and exception to copyright applies (see the relevant FAQ at *https://creativecommons.org/faq/#do-creative-commons-licenses-affect-exceptions-and-limitations-to-copyright-such-as-fair-dealing-and-fair-use*).
- When the work is in the public domain (see the relevant FAQ[1] at *https://creativecommons.org/faq/#may-i-apply-a-creative-commons-license-to-a-work-in-the-public-domain*).

BECAUSE USERS DON'T NEED COPYRIGHT LICENSES IN THESE SCENARIOS, CC LICENSES AREN'T NEEDED

Can you think of reasons why someone might try to apply a CC license to a work that is not covered by copyright in their own country? Or reasons why a CC licensor might expect attribution every time their work is used, even for a use that is not prohibited by copyright law?

These users might be trying to exert control that they do not actually have by law. But more likely than not, they simply don't know that copyright does not apply, or that a work is in the public domain. Or, for the savvy licensor, they may realize that their work is in the public domain in some countries but not everywhere, and they want to be sure that everyone everywhere will be able to reuse it.

For a real-life example, let's look at what happens when you want to use CC licenses in a field like 3D printing. Look at the resource provided by Public Knowledge (licensed CC BY-SA 3.0, available at https://www.publicknowledge .org/assets/uploads/documents/3_Steps_for_Licensing_Your_3D_Printed_Stuff .pdf) about how to apply a CC license in the 3D printing field. It is easy to see how complicated the legal issues can become, particularly in newly emerging fields like this one.

One other subtle but important difference about the scope of CC licenses is that they also cover other rights that are closely related to copyright. These are defined as "Similar Rights" in the CC license legal code, and they include related and neighboring rights and what are known as "sui genesis database rights," which are rights in some countries restricting the extraction and reuse of the contents of a database. See section 2.1 "Copyright Basics" for a refresher on what Similar Rights covers. Just as with copyright, the CC license conditions only come into play when Similar Rights otherwise apply to the work *and* to the particular reuse made by someone using the CC-licensed work.

The other critical part of the statement "CC licenses are copyright licenses" is that there may be other rights in a work upon which the license has no effect— for example, privacy rights. Again, CC licenses do not have any effect on rights beyond copyright and Similar Rights as defined in the licenses, so other rights have to be managed separately. Read the FAQ about this issue at https://creative commons.org/faq/#does-a-creative-commons-license-give-me-all-the-rights-i -need-to-use-the-work.

While it is not required, Creative Commons urges creators to make sure that there are no other rights that may prevent the reuse of their work as intended. CC licensors do not make any warranties about the reuse of the work. This means that unless the licensor is offering a separate warranty, it is incumbent on the reuser to determine whether other rights may impact their intended reuse of the work. Learning more about this can sometimes be as easy as contacting the licensor to inquire about these possible other rights. Read through the complete list of considerations for licensees of CC-licensed works, licensed CC BY 4.0, at https://wiki.creativecommons.org/wiki/Considerations_for _licensors_and_licensees#Considerations_for_licensees.

WHAT TYPES OF CONTENT CAN BE CC-LICENSED?

You can apply a CC license to anything protected by copyright that you own, with one important exception.

CC urges creators *not* to apply CC licenses to software. This is because there are many free and open-source software licenses which do that job better; they were built specifically as software licenses. For example, most open-source software licenses include provisions about distributing the software's source code—but the CC licenses do not address this important aspect of sharing software. The software-sharing ecosystem is well established, and there are many good open-source software licenses to choose from. An FAQ from Creative Commons' website available at https://creativecommons.org/faq/#can-i-apply-a-creative-commons-license-to-software has more information about why we discourage the use of our licenses for software.

WHOSE RIGHTS ARE COVERED BY THE CC LICENSE?

A CC license on a given work only covers the copyright held by the person who applied the license—the licensor. This might sound obvious, but it is an important point to understand. For example, many employers own the copyright to works created by their employees, so if an employee applies a CC license to a work owned by their employer, they are not able to give any permission whatsoever to reuse the work. The person who applies the license needs to be either the creator or someone who has acquired the rights to the work.

Additionally, a work may incorporate the copyrighted work of another, such as a scholarly article that uses a copyrighted photograph to illustrate an idea (after having received the permission of the owner of the photograph to include it). The CC license applied by the author of the scholarly article does not apply to the photograph, only to the remainder of the work. Separate permission may need to be obtained in order to reproduce the photograph (but not the remainder of the article). See section 3.4 "License Enforceability" for more details on how to handle these situations.

Also, works often have more than one copyright attached to them. For example, a filmmaker may own the copyright to a film adaptation of a book, but the book author also holds a copyright to the book on which the film is based. In this example, if the film is CC-licensed, the CC license only applies to the film and not the book. The user may need to separately obtain a license to use the copyrightable content from the book that is part of the film.

Final Remarks

A key to understanding how Creative Commons works is understanding that the licenses depend on copyright to function. This seemingly simple concept explains a lot about when the tools apply and how much of a work they cover.

3.3 | LICENSE TYPES

There are six different CC licenses, which are designed to help accommodate the diverse needs of creators while still using simple, standardized terms.

LEARNING OUTCOMES
- Explain the CC license suite
- Describe the different CC license elements

THE BIG QUESTION: WHY IT MATTERS
Why are there so many different Creative Commons licenses?

There is no single Creative Commons license. The CC license suite (which includes the six CC licenses) and the CC0 Public Domain Dedication offer creators a range of options. At first, all of these choices can appear daunting. But when you dig into the options, you will realize that the spectrum of choices is fairly simple.

PERSONAL REFLECTION: WHY IT MATTERS TO YOU
Think about a piece of creative or academic work you made that you are particularly proud of. If you shared that work with others, would you have been okay with them adapting it or using it for commercial purposes? Why or why not?

Acquiring Essential Knowledge

Creative Commons licenses are standardized tools, but part of the vision is to provide a range of options for creators who are interested in sharing their works with the public rather than reserving all rights under copyright.

The four license elements—BY, SA, NC, and ND—combine to make up six different license options.

All of the licenses include the BY condition. In other words, all of the licenses require that the creator be attributed in connection with their work. Beyond that commonality, the licenses vary as to whether (1) commercial use of the work is permitted, and (2) whether the work can be adapted or modified, and if so, on what terms.

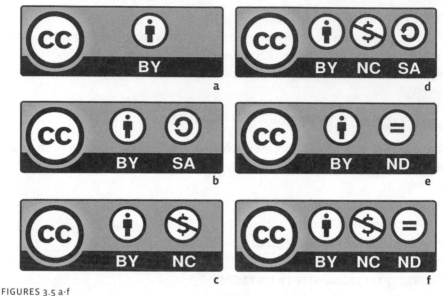

FIGURES 3.5 a-f
The six BY licenses

The six licenses, from least to most restrictive in terms of the freedoms granted reusers, are shown in figures 3.5a to 3.5f.

The *Attribution* license, or *CC BY* (figure 3.5a), allows people to use the work for any purpose (even commercially and even in modified form) as long as they give attribution to the creator.

The *Attribution-ShareAlike* license, or *BY-SA* (figure 3.5b), allows people to use the work for any purpose (even commercially and even in modified form), as long as they give attribution to the creator and make any adaptations they share with others available under the same or a compatible license. This is Creative Commons' version of a copyleft license (a type of open source software license that makes the license permissions viral by design), and is the license required for the content uploaded to *Wikipedia*, for example.

The *Attribution-NonCommercial* license, or *BY-NC* (figure 3.5c), allows people to use the work for noncommercial purposes only, and only as long as they give attribution to the creator.

The *Attribution-NonCommercial-ShareAlike* license, or *BY-NC-SA* (figure 3.5d), allows people to use the work for noncommercial purposes only, and only as long as they give attribution to the creator and make any adaptations they share with others available under the same or a compatible license.

The *Attribution-NoDerivatives* license, or *BY-ND* (figure 3.5e), allows people to use the unadapted work for any purpose (even commercially), as long as they give attribution to the creator. But they cannot use adapted or modified versions of the work (these are called "derivatives").

The *Attribution-NonCommercial-NoDerivatives* license, or *BY-NC-ND* (figure 3.5f), is the most restrictive license offered by Creative Commons. It allows people to use the unadapted work for noncommercial purposes only, and only as long as they give attribution to the licensor. Adaptations or modified versions of the work are not permitted.

To really understand how the different license options work, let's dig into the different license elements. Attribution is a part of all CC licenses, and we will dissect exactly what type of attribution is required in chapter 4. For now, let's focus on what makes the licenses different.

COMMERCIAL VS. NONCOMMERCIAL USE
Noncommercial (NC)

As we know, three of the licenses (BY-NC, BY-NC-SA, and BY-NC-ND) limit reuse of the work to noncommercial purposes only. In the legal code, a noncommercial purpose is defined as one that is "not primarily intended for or directed towards commercial advantage or monetary compensation." This phrasing is intended to provide flexibility depending on the facts surrounding the reuse, without overly specifying exact situations that could exclude some prohibited and some permitted reuses.

It is important to note that CC's definition of NC depends on the use, not the user. If you are a nonprofit or charitable organization, your use of an NC-licensed work could still run afoul of the NC restriction, and if you are a for-profit entity, your use of an NC-licensed work does not necessarily mean you have violated the license terms. For example, a nonprofit entity cannot sell another's NC-licensed work for a profit, and a for-profit entity may use an NC-licensed work for noncommercial purposes. Whether a use is commercial depends on the specifics of the situation. See our CC "NonCommercial Interpretation" page, licensed CC BY 4.0, at https://wiki.creativecommons.org/wiki/NonCommercial _interpretation for more information and examples.

ADAPTATIONS

The other differences between the licenses hinge on whether, and on what terms, reusers can adapt and then share the licensed work. The question of what constitutes an adaptation of a licensed work depends on applicable copyright law (for a reminder, see chapter 2). One of the exclusive rights granted to creators under copyright is the right to create adaptations or modified versions of their works or, as they are sometimes called, "derivative works." Examples of these adaptations include creating a movie based on a book or translating a book from one language to another.

As a legal matter, at times it is tricky to determine exactly what is and is not an adaptation. Here are some handy rules about the licenses to keep in mind:

Technical format-shifting (for example, converting a licensed work from a digital format to a physical copy) is *not* an adaptation regardless of what the applicable copyright law may otherwise provide.

- Fixing minor problems with spelling or punctuation is not an adaptation.
- Syncing a musical work with a moving image *is* an adaptation regardless of what the applicable copyright law may otherwise provide.
- Reproducing and putting works together into a collection is *not* an adaptation of the individual works. For example, combining stand-alone essays by several authors into an essay collection for use as an open textbook is a collection and *not* an adaptation. Most open courseware is a collection of others' open educational resources (OER).
- Including an image in connection with text, as in a blog post, a PowerPoint, or an article, does not create an adaptation unless the photo itself is adapted.

NoDerivatives

Two of the CC licenses (BY-ND and BY-NC-ND) prohibit reusers from sharing (i.e., distributing or making available) adaptations of the licensed work. To be clear, this means that anyone may create adaptations of works under an ND license so long as they don't share the work with others in adapted form. This allows, among other things, organizations to engage in text and data mining without violating the ND term.

ShareAlike

Two of the licenses (BY-SA and BY-NC-SA) require that if adaptations of the licensed work are shared, they must be made available under the same or a compatible license. For ShareAlike purposes, the list of compatible licenses is short. It includes later versions of the same license (e.g., BY-SA 4.0 is compatible with BY-SA 3.0) and a few non-CC licenses designated as compatible by Creative Commons (e.g., the Free Art License). You can read more about this at the CC wiki ShareAlike Compatibility page, licensed CC BY 4.0, available at_https://wiki.creativecommons.org/wiki/ShareAlike_compatibility, but the most important thing to remember is that ShareAlike requires that if you share your adaptation, you must do so using the same or a compatible license.

Public Domain

In addition to the CC license suite, Creative Commons also has an option for creators who want to take a "no rights reserved" approach and disclaim copyright entirely. This is CC0, the Public Domain Dedication tool.

Like the CC licenses, CC0 (read "CC Zero") uses the three-layer design—legal code, deed, and metadata. The CC0 legal code itself uses a three-pronged legal approach. The first approach is for the creator to simply waive all of their rights to the work. But some countries do not allow creators to dedicate their work to the public domain through a waiver or abandonment of their rights, so CC0 includes a "fallback" license that allows anyone in the world to do anything with the work unconditionally. The fallback license comes into play when the waiver fails for any reason. And finally, in the rare instance that both the waiver and the "fallback" license are not enforceable, CC includes a promise by the person applying CC0 to their work that they will not assert copyright against reusers in a manner that interferes with their stated intention of surrendering all rights in the work.

Like the licenses, CC0 is a copyright tool, but it also covers a few additional rights beyond those covered by the CC licenses, such as noncompetition laws. From a reuse perspective, there still may be other rights that require clearance separately, such as trademark and patent rights, and third-party rights in the work, such as publicity or privacy rights.

Final Remarks

Creative Commons legal tools were designed to provide a solution to complicated laws in a standardized way, making them as easy as possible for non-lawyers to use and apply. Understanding the basic legal principles in this section will help you use the CC licenses and public domain tools more effectively.

3.4 | LICENSE ENFORCEABILITY

Creative Commons licenses have been carefully crafted to make them legally enforceable in countries around the world.

LEARNING OUTCOMES
- Describe the state of Creative Commons case law
- Explain the potential benefits of seeking nonlegal resolutions to disagreements

THE BIG QUESTION: WHY IT MATTERS

Creative Commons licenses are legal tools that build on copyright law. As legal instruments, CC licenses need to stand up in court. What happens when there is a court case that involves CC licenses? What happens if someone is violating the CC license you applied to a work, but you don't want to file a lawsuit? What happens if a licensor complains about how you have attributed them when reusing their work?

To date and to our knowledge, no court around the world that has heard a case involving a CC license (and there have been very few such cases) has questioned the validity or enforceability of a CC license. Thanks to the Creative Commons community, most disputes connected to CC licenses are resolved outside of court and often without involving lawyers.

PERSONAL REFLECTION: WHY IT MATTERS TO YOU

Whether you or your organization are using CC licenses, or you're advising others in the use of such licenses, you want to be confident that the terms of those licenses are enforceable. If someone misuses your work, what recourse do you have? What would you do if you found out that someone was using your CC-licensed photograph in a magazine without giving you credit, for example?

Acquiring Essential Knowledge

Most people who reuse CC-licensed works try to comply with the license conditions. But whether well-meaning or not, sometimes people get it wrong.

If someone is using a CC-licensed work without giving attribution or otherwise following the license, their right to use the work ends automatically as soon as they violate the license terms. Unless the person using the work received separate permission or is relying upon fair use or some other exception to copyright, they are potentially liable for copyright infringement. To learn what happens when someone does not comply with a CC license, read the FAQ at https://creativecommons.org/faq/#what-happens-if-i-offer-my-material -under-a-creative-commons-license-and-someone-misuses-them. For a look at what happens from the perspective of a reuser, read the FAQ at https://creative commons.org/faq/#how-can-i-lose-my-rights-under-a-creative-commons -license-if-that-happens-how-do-i-get-them-back.

Note this important difference between the newest version of CC licenses (Version 4.0) and prior versions in the text box below:

30-day window to correct license violations

All CC licenses terminate when a licensee breaks their terms, but under 4.0, a licensee's rights are reinstated automatically if she corrects a breach within 30 days of discovering it. The cure period in version 4.0 resembles similar provisions in some other public licenses and better reflects how licensors and licensees resolve compliance issues in practice. It also assures users that provided they act promptly, they can continue using the CC-licensed work without worry that they may have lost their rights permanently.

Under Version 4.0, users of CC-licensed works who come into compliance with license terms within thirty days of discovering they were in violation of the terms have their rights under the license automatically reinstated.

FIGURE 3.6 **What's new in Version 4.0 of the CC licenses?**
From the "What's New in 4.0 Page" on the Creative Commons website: https:// creativecommons.org/share-your-work/licensing-considerations/version4/ *CC BY 4.0*

Sometimes these types of disputes can end up in court. Over the course of Creative Commons' history, to our knowledge, there have been very few legal disputes and decisions involving CC legal tools. Each court that has rendered a decision has made it without questioning the enforceability of the CC license at issue.

Those judicial decisions have been in a variety of places around the world, including Spain, Belgium, Netherlands, Germany, Sweden, Israel, and the United States. Creative Commons maintains a listing of court decisions and case law from jurisdictions around the world on its wiki, licensed CC BY 4.0, available at https://wiki.creativecommons.org/wiki/Case_Law.

In all of these decisions, no court has questioned the validity of a CC license in the case. While a CC license played a minor role in some of the cases, in others the court has held the defendant liable for copyright infringement for failing to follow the CC license terms. You can read about one such decision at the CC wiki page Curry v. Audax, licensed CC BY 4.0 and available at https://wiki.creative commons.org/wiki/Curry_v._Audax.

Legal enforceability is one of the key features of CC licensing. While the licenses are widely seen as symbols of free and open sharing, they also carry legal weight. The CC legal code was written by lawyers with the help of a global network of international copyright experts. The result is a set of terms and conditions that are intended to operate and be enforceable everywhere in the world.

LICENSE VERSIONS

As noted above, there are different *versions* of CC licenses. These are not to be confused with the different *types* of licenses described in section 3.3. The license version number simply represents when that particular version of the CC legal code was written. Creative Commons improves its licenses through the process of versioning, by which we update the legal code to better account for changes in copyright law and technology, and the needs of reusers. While there are some differences between license versions, the different versions are largely the same in practical effect. The latest version of the CC license suite is Version 4.0, which was published in 2013. Details on what updates were made to the licenses in Version 4.0 can be found at https://creativecommons.org/share -your-work/licensing-considerations/version4. For the most definitive and comprehensive view of how the licenses have changed from Version 1.0 to the present, including all changes to the attribution and marking requirements, visit the CC wiki page, licensed CC BY 4.0, available at https://wiki.creativecommons .org/wiki/License_Versions.

In all cases, we recommend that creators use the latest version of the licenses, because it reflects the latest thinking of Creative Commons and its global network of legal experts.

OFFICIAL TRANSLATIONS OF CC LEGAL TOOLS

The latest versions of all the CC licenses (and other tools) may be translated into official versions in other languages. Creative Commons has a formal process (see the Legal Code Translation Policy, licensed CC BY 4.0 and available at https://wiki.creativecommons.org/wiki/Legal_Code_Translation_Policy) by which this is done in order to ensure that the translations are as close to the original as possible. Creative Commons' goal is to get the licenses into as many languages as possible, so that everyone can read and understand the terms in their native language. The official translations are noted at the bottom of the legal code on all of the licenses and are equivalents of one another.

Many people ask about the relationship between the official translations and the English originals. All official translations are linguistic translations only, unlike ported versions (which are described in the text box below). The official translations are legal equivalents of one another, which means they have the same legal meaning and effect in each language. This is similar to how standards bodies such as the World Wide Web Consortium translate a single standard into many different languages, and how the United Nations publishes treaties.

RESOLVING DISPUTES

Since the publication of Version 1.0 of the licenses in 2002, Creative Commons is aware of a relatively small number of disputes between licensors and reusers over its licenses, including the NonCommercial term and attribution. There may be several explanations for this state of harmony. As observed by Creative Commons in its "Defining 'Noncommercial'" report (licensed CC BY 3.0 and

---

Distinguishing ported versions of the pre-4.0 versions of the CC licenses.

Prior to the publication of Version 4.0 in November 2013, Creative Commons gave permission to the CC Global Network to "port" the Creative Commons licenses. Porting involved linguistic translation and adjustments so that the licenses reflected local terminology and drafting protocols, and it accounted for other local differences, such as the existence of moral rights and collecting societies.

One of the primary reasons for versioning the licenses from 3.0 to 4.0 was to eliminate the need for porting, an unnecessarily complex process that could be eliminated if Creative Commons took proper care to ensure that the new licenses were internationalized. Starting with Version 4.0, the most recent version of the CC license suite, Creative Commons no longer "ports" the licenses. The ported licenses of previous versions may still be used and remain legally valid and enforceable; however, Creative Commons discourages their use and recommends Version 4.0 as the latest and most up-to-date thinking of CC and its global network.

available at https://mirrors.creativecommons.org/defining-noncommercial/ Defining_Noncommercial_fullreport.pdf), the expectations of licensors and reusers of CC-licensed content may play a role here. For example, NC licensors often intend for broad reuse of their NC-licensed content, as long as it is not reused primarily for commercial gain. However, the reusers of NC-licensed content may assume more conservative license terms around commercial reuse. As a result, NC-licensed content is not often reused to the full extent of the permissions that the license affords or the licensor intends. And often, when disputes around CC-licensed content do arise, they are resolved amicably and out of court, frequently without involving lawyers. Instead, disputes are resolved through outreach by the licensor to the user, and an accord is struck to fix any actual problem.

Note that Creative Commons accounted for this practice in Version 4.0. Whereas prior to 4.0, any violation of the license automatically terminated the license, and the violator had to seek new and express permission from the licensor to reuse the work again, in Version 4.0, the license automatically reinstates if the violator corrects the problem within thirty days of having become aware of it. This encourages reusers to do the right thing—correct their violations as soon as possible upon discovery, whether or not the licensor has made a claim. This can help avoid disputes.

In many ways, both of these practices—being more generous and respectful, and outreach to solve any perceived violations—are a testament to the values held and practiced by the CC community of creators and reusers. Creative Commons encourages healthy, open interactions between licensors and those reusing their works.

Final Remarks

The legal robustness of the CC licenses is critically important. With the help of an international network of legal and policy experts, the CC licenses are accepted and enforceable worldwide. To date, no court has declared the licenses unenforceable, and very few lawsuits have ensued. In the vast majority of cases, the CC community has resolved any disputes outside of the courtroom.

3.5 | ADDITIONAL RESOURCES

- "About the Open Publication License," by David Wiley. CC BY 4.0.
  A brief history that outlines open content licensing and why the licenses were eventually replaced by the more robust Creative Commons licenses: http://opencontent.org/blog/archives/329.

- "Creative Commons License," *Wikipedia* article. CC BY-SA 3.0.
  This *Wikipedia* article explains the CC licenses and some use instructions: https://en.wikipedia.org/wiki/Creative_Commons_license.

- "About the Licenses," by Creative Commons. CC BY 4.0.
  To read all of the CC license deeds and legal codes, visit this site and explore the different licenses: https://creativecommons.org/licenses/.

Selected Frequently Asked Questions by Creative Commons (CC BY 4.0)

- *Do Creative Commons licenses affect the exceptions and limitations to copyright, such as fair dealing and fair use? See* https://creativecommons.org/faq/#do-creative-commons-licenses-affect-exceptions-and-limitations-to-copyright-such-as-fair-dealing-and-fair-use.

- *May I apply a Creative Commons license to a work in the public domain? See* https://creativecommons.org/faq/#may-i-apply-a-creative-commons-license-to-a-work-in-the-public-domain.

- *What happens if I offer my material under a Creative Commons license and someone misuses that material? See* https://creativecommons.org/faq/#what-happens-if-i-offer-my-material-under-a-creative-commons-license-and-someone-misuses-them.

- *How can I lose my rights under a Creative Commons license? If that happens, how do I get them back? See* https://creativecommons.org/faq/#how-can-i-lose-my-rights-under-a-creative-commons-license-if-that-happens-how-do-i-get-them-back.

Participants' Recommended Resources

CC Certificate participants have recommended many additional resources through Hypothes.is annotations on the Certificate website. While Creative Commons has not vetted these resources, we wanted to highlight participants' suggestions here: https://certificates.creativecommons.org/cccerteducomments/chapter/additional-resources-3/.

NOTE

1. Remember that the term of copyright for works varies around the world. So, in some situations, a work may be in the public domain under the laws of Uganda but not in the public domain under the laws of Indonesia. This means that depending on the law that applies to your use (generally, where you are when using the work), the CC license may or may not apply.

Using CC Licenses and CC-Licensed Works

NOW THAT YOU KNOW HOW THE CC LICENSES WORK AND HOW THEY ARE designed, you are ready to use CC licenses and CC0 for your own work, and reuse CC-licensed works created by others.

This chapter covers what you need to know as a CC licensor and as a reuser. When your own CC-licensed work incorporates CC-licensed work made by others, you are both!

This chapter has five sections:

1. Choosing and Applying a CC License
2. Things to Consider after CC Licensing
3. Finding and Reusing CC-Licensed Work
4. Remixing CC-Licensed Work
5. Additional Resources

4.1 | CHOOSING AND APPLYING A CC LICENSE

The act of applying a CC license is easy, but there are several important considerations to think through before you do.

FIGURE 4.1 **CC BY License Icon**

CC BY License Button. Trademark: Creative Commons.

LEARNING OUTCOMES
- Name the most important considerations before applying a CC license or CC0
- Apply a license using CC's License Chooser and a CC0 using CC's Public Domain Dedication
- Evaluate which license to apply based on the relevant factors

THE BIG QUESTION: WHY IT MATTERS
What should creators consider before applying a CC license or CC0 to their work? There are several options for creators who choose to share their work by using CC. There are also many things to think about before applying any CC license or CC0, including whether you have all the rights you need and if not, how you must indicate that to the public.

PERSONAL REFLECTION: WHY IT MATTERS TO YOU
How would you go about choosing a particular CC license for your work? Do you know how to go about actually attaching a license to your work once you have chosen one? What if you change your mind about the license?

Acquiring Essential Knowledge
Before you decide that you want to apply a CC license or CC0 to your creative work, there are some important things to consider:

- *The licenses and CC0 are irrevocable.* The word *irrevocable* means that a legal agreement cannot be canceled. This means that once you apply a CC license to a work, that license applies to the work until the copyright on the work expires. This aspect of CC licensing is highly desirable from the perspective of reusers because they can be confident that the creator cannot arbitrarily pull back the rights granted them under the CC license.
  - » Because the licenses are irrevocable, it is very important to carefully consider your options before deciding to apply a CC license to a work.

- *You must own or control copyright in the work.* You should control copyright in the work to which you apply the CC license. For example, you don't own or control any copyright in a work that is in the public domain, and you don't own or control the copyright to an Enrique Iglesias song. Furthermore, if you created the material in the scope of your employment, you may not be the holder of the rights and may need to get permission from your employer before applying a CC license to it. Before licensing, be mindful about whether you have copyright to the work to which you're applying a CC license.

WHICH CREATIVE COMMONS LICENSE SHOULD I USE?

The six CC licenses provide a range of options for creators who want to share their work with the public while still retaining copyright. The best way to decide which license is appropriate for you is to think about why you want to share your work, and how you hope others will use that work.

For example, here are a few questions to consider:

- Do you think people might make interesting new works out of your creation? Do you want to give people the ability to translate your writing into different languages, or otherwise customize it for their own needs? If so, then you should choose a license that allows your work to be adapted.
- Is it important to you that your images are able to be incorporated into *Wikipedia*? If so, then you should choose either CC BY, BY-SA, or CC0, because *Wikipedia* does not allow images licensed under any of the Non-Commercial or NoDerivatives licenses except in limited circumstances.
- Do you want to give away all of your rights in your work so that it can be used by anyone in the world for any purpose? Then you might want to think about using the Public Domain Dedication tool, CC0.

If you need some help deciding which license might be best for you, this flow-chart from CC Australia might be useful (please note that the information it contains is not legal advice): see figure 4.2 or go to http://creativecommons.org.au/lcarn/fact-sheets/licensing-flowchart/.

HOW DO I APPLY A CC LICENSE TO MY WORK?

Once you've decided you want to use a CC license and know which license you want to use, applying it is simple. Technically, all you have to do is indicate which CC license you are applying to your work. However, we strongly recommend including a link (or writing out the CC license URL, if you are working offline) to the relevant CC license deed (e.g., https://creativecommons.org/licenses/by/4.0). You can do this in the copyright notice for your work, on the

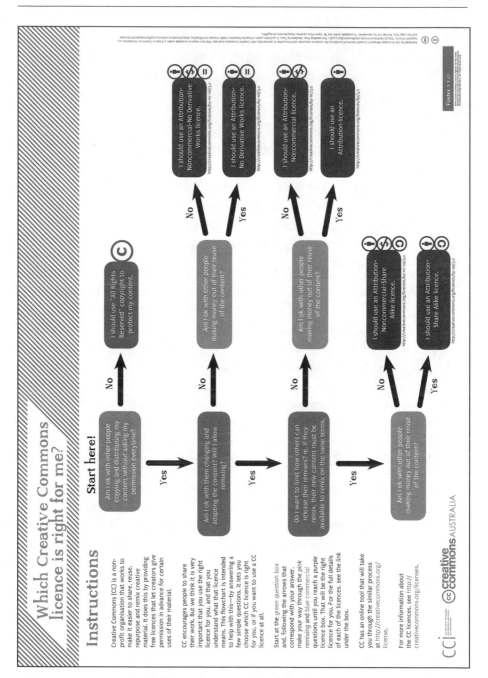

FIGURE 4.2 **Which Creative Commons license is right for me?**

Image from Creative Commons Australia: http://creativecommons.org.au/learn/fact-sheets/
licensing-flowchart/

Author: CC Australia | CC BY 3.0 | Desaturated from original

FIGURE 4.3 **Screenshot of the footer of BC Open Textbooks**

footer of your website, or any other place that makes sense in light of the particular format and medium of your work. The important thing is to make it clear what the CC license covers and locate the notice in a place which makes that clear to the public. See "Marking Your Work with a CC License" (licensed CC BY 4.0 and available at https://wiki.creativecommons.org/wiki/Marking_your_work _with_a_CC_license) on the Creative Commons website for more information.

Indicating which CC license you choose can be as simple as the notice from the footer of BC Open Textbooks (https://open.bccampus.ca/find-open-textbooks), shown in figure 4.3.

If you are on a platform like Medium or Flickr, you should use the built-in CC license tools on the platform to mark your work with the CC license you choose.

If you have a personal blog or a website, we recommend using the *CC license chooser* to generate code that identifies your chosen license. That code can be copied and inserted into your work online.

You should take some time to play around with the CC license chooser, at https://creativecommons.org/choose/, now (figure 4.4). After you select the boxes that indicate your preferences, the chooser generates the appropriate license based on your selections. Remember, the license chooser is not a registration page, it simply provides you with standardized HTML code, icons and license statements.

In figure 4.4, do you see the text and icon just above the code? That text/links can also be copied and pasted onto your work to mark the work with a CC license.

If you want to mark the work in a different way or need to use a different format like closing titles in a video, you can visit https://creativecommons.org/about/downloads/ and access downloadable versions of all of the CC icons.

How to Apply a CC0 License

Like the licenses, CC0 has its own chooser. If you want to dedicate your work to the public domain, you can go to https://creativecommons.org/choose/zero/waiver. Complete the required fields, agree to the terms, and then get the metadata to mark your work with a CC0 license.

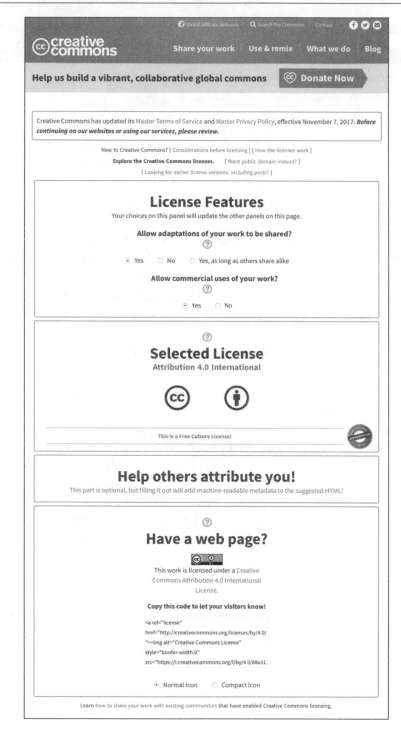

FIGURE 4.4   **CC License Chooser**

Whatever method you use to mark your content, there are several important steps for proper CC license marking. Here are three cases in which you will mark CC-licensed works:

1. *Marking your own work* so that others can easily discover it, reuse it, and give you credit or attribution. The best practice for marking your work is to follow the TASL approach for your own portions of the content, and for the portions of the content created by others:

   » T = Title
   » A = Author (tell reusers who to give credit to)
   » S = Source (give reusers a link to the resource)
   » L = License (provide a link to the CC license deed)

   When providing attribution, the goal is to mark the work with full TASL information. When you don't have some of the TASL information about a work, do the best you can and include as much detail as possible in the marking statement.

   You should note that starting with Version 4.0, the licenses no longer require a reuser to include the title as part of the attribution statement. However, if the title is provided, then Creative Commons encourages you to include it when attributing the author.

   For more examples of how to mark your own work in different contexts, spend some time looking through Creative Commons' extensive marking page "Marking Your Work with a CC License" (licensed CC BY 4.0 and available at https://wiki.creativecommons.org/wiki/Marking _your_work_with_a_CC_license). See the caption of figure 4.5 as an example of marking an image with TASL information. It is a good example of CC marking because TASL with all appropriate links is provided in the attribution statement.

2. *Indicating if your work is based on someone else's work.* If your work is a modification or adaptation of another work, you should indicate this and provide attribution to the creator of the original work. You should also include a link to the work you modified and indicate what license applies to that work. Figure 4.6 is an example of this.

3. *Marking work created by others* that you are incorporating into your own work. Figure 4.7 is an example here from a Saylor Academy course.

FIGURE 4.5
Creative Commons 10th birthday celebration in San Francisco

*Image from Flickr: flickr.com/photos/
sixteenmilesofstring/8256206923*
Author: tvol | CC BY 2.0
Desaturated from original

This work, "90fied," is a derivate of "Creative Commons 10th Birthday Celebration San Francisco" (flickr.com/photos/sixteenmilesofstring/8256206923) by tvol (*https://www.flickr.com/photos/sixteenmilesofstring/*), used under CC BY (*https://creativecommons.org/licenses/by/2.0/*). "90fied" is licensed under CC BY by [Your name here].

FIGURE 4.6
Example of a modification of another work and the attribution you would apply

Desaturated from original

In every case, the goals are the same: you want to make it easy for others to know who created which parts of the work. To do this, you should (1) identify the terms under which any given work, or part of a work, can be used, and (2) provide information about the works you used to create your new work or that you incorporated into your work.

Final Remarks

When applying a CC license to a work, you should (1) use the *CC license chooser* to determine which CC license best meets your needs. Apply the license code if possible, or copy and paste the text and links provided. (2) If you are using an online platform, use the built-in CC license tools to mark your work with a CC license. (3) Mark your work and give proper attribution to others' works using the TASL approach.

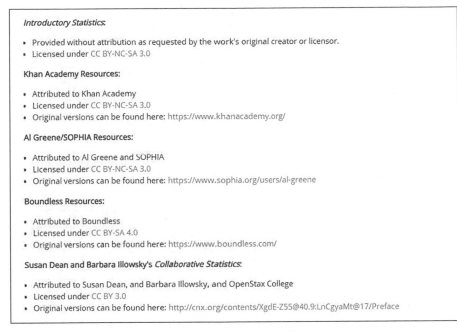

FIGURE 4.7 **Example of marking works created by others**

There is no single answer for which CC license is the best one for your work. It is important to remember why you are sharing your work and what you hope others might do with it, before making your CC license choice.

4.2 | THINGS TO CONSIDER AFTER CC LICENSING

Applying a CC license alone is not enough to ensure that your work is freely available for easy reuse and remix. Licensors must also consider additional factors that affect the accessibility and usability of their works for future users.

LEARNING OUTCOMES
- Explain why CC discourages changing the license terms
- Explain how a paywall affects CC-licensed content
- Describe why the technical format of content is significant
- Describe what happens when someone changes their mind about CC licensing

THE BIG QUESTION: WHY IT MATTERS

One of the most important aspects of Creative Commons licenses is that they are standardized. This makes it much easier for the public to understand how the licenses work and what reusers have to do to meet their obligations.

But CC licenses do not apply to works in a vacuum. CC-licensed works usually live on websites that have their own terms of service. Or sometimes, these works are not in formats that make it easy to reuse or adapt them. And the works are often available in hard-copy form for a price.

PERSONAL REFLECTION: WHY IT MATTERS TO YOU

Have you ever found a CC-licensed work that you weren't easily able to copy and share? What made it hard to reuse as intended? Was it an issue of technical format, or were there access restrictions on the work, or something else?

Acquiring Essential Knowledge

Creative Commons licenses are standardized licenses, which means the terms and conditions are the same for all works subject to the same type of CC license. This is an essential feature of their design, enabling the public to remix CC-licensed works. It also makes the licenses easy to understand.

But people and institutions that use the licenses have diverse needs and wants. Sometimes creators want slightly different terms rather than the standard terms that CC licenses offer.

Creative Commons strongly discourages people from customizing open copyright licenses because this creates confusion, requires users to take the time to learn about how the custom license differs, and eliminates the benefits of standardization. If you change any of the terms and conditions of a CC license, you cannot call it a Creative Commons license or otherwise use the CC trademarks. This rule also applies if you try to add restrictions on what people can do with CC-licensed work through your separate agreements, such as website terms of service. For example, your website's terms of service can't tell people they can't copy a CC-licensed work (if they are complying with the license terms). You can, however, make your CC-licensed work available on more *permissive* terms and still call it a CC license. For example, you may waive your right to receive attribution.

Creative Commons has a detailed legal policy, Modifying the CC Licenses, (licensed CC BY 4.0 and available at https://wiki.creativecommons.org/wiki/Modifying_the_CC_licenses) which outlines these rules. However, the best way to apply them is to ask yourself: "Is what I want to do going to make it easier or harder for people to use my CC-licensed work?" If the latter, then generally it's a restriction and you can't do it unless you remove the Creative Commons name from the work.

Note that all of the above applies to creators of CC-licensed work. You can never change the legal terms that apply to someone else's CC-licensed work.

CHARGING FOR A CC-LICENSED WORK

The first part of this section dealt with the requirements connected to changing the legal terms on a CC-licensed work, whether by actually changing the license terms or using separate contracts to try to do so.

But what if you simply want to sell a CC-licensed work?

If you are the creator, then selling your work is always okay. In fact, selling physical copies (e.g., a textbook) and providing digital copies for free is a very common method for making money while using CC licenses.

Figure 4.8 highlights Cards Against Humanity, a card game available under a Creative Commons BY-NC-SA 2.0 license. Cards Against Humanity offers their cards decks online for free download but sells physical copies.

Charging for access to *digital* copies of a CC-licensed work is more difficult. It is permissible, but once someone pays for a copy of your work, they can legally distribute it to others for free under the terms of the applicable CC license.

FIGURE 4.8 **Stack of Cards Against Humanity packs**
Photo from Flickr: flickr.com/photos/jareed/9669594018/
Author: jareed | CC BY 2.0 | Desaturated from original

If you are charging for access to someone else's CC-licensed work—whether a physical copy or digital version—you have to pay attention to the particular CC license applied to the work. If the CC license includes the NonCommercial (NC) restriction, then you cannot charge the public to access the work.

MAKING YOUR WORK ACCESSIBLE

Formats: Simply applying a CC license to a creative work does not necessarily make it easy for others to reuse and remix it. Think about what technical format you are using for your content (e.g., PDF or MP3). Can people download your work? Can they easily edit or remix it if the license allows? In addition to the final polished version, many creators distribute editable source files of their content to make it easier for those who want to use the work for their own purposes. For example, in addition to the physical book or e-book, you might want to distribute files of a CC-licensed book that enable people to easily cut and paste the content into their own works.

DRM: Using a distribution platform that applies digital rights management (DRM), such as copy protection technology, to your work is another way you can inadvertently make it very hard for reusers to make use of the permissions in the CC license. If you have to upload your CC-licensed works to a platform that uses DRM, you should consider also distributing the same content on sites that do not use DRM.

Note that the CC licenses prohibit you from applying DRM to someone else's CC-licensed work without their permission.

WHAT IF YOU CHANGE YOUR MIND ABOUT THE CC LICENSE?

Inevitably, there are creators who apply a CC license to a work and then later decide they want to offer that work on different terms. Even though the original license cannot be revoked, the creator is free to *also* offer the work under a different license. Similarly, the creator is free to remove the copy of the work that they placed online.

In these cases, anyone who finds the work under the original license is legally permitted to use it under those terms until the copyright expires. But as a practical matter, reusers may want to comply with the creator's new wishes as a matter of respect.

WHAT IF SOMEONE DOES SOMETHING WITH MY CC-LICENSED WORK I DON'T LIKE?

As long as users abide by the license terms and conditions, authors/licensors cannot control how their material is used. That said, all CC licenses provide several mechanisms that allow licensors to choose not to be associated with their material, or to uses of their material with which they disagree.

- First, all CC licenses prohibit using the attribution requirement to suggest that the licensor endorses or supports a particular use.
- Second, licensors may waive the attribution requirement, choosing not to be identified as the licensor, if they wish.
- Third, if the licensor does not like how the material has been modified or used, CC licenses require that the licensee remove the attribution information upon request. (In Version 3.0 and earlier, this is only a requirement for adaptations and collections; in 4.0, this also applies to the unmodified work.)
- Finally, anyone modifying licensed material must indicate that the original has been modified. This ensures that changes made to the original material—whether or not the licensor approves of them—are not attributed back to the licensor.
- Furthermore, it is important to remember that:
  » The Commons is full of good people who want to do the right thing, so we rarely see much "abuse" of openly licensed works. Using CC licenses gives good, responsible people the freedom to use and build on your work.
  » Copyright and/or open copyright licenses don't keep "bad" people from doing "bad" things with your work if they don't care about copyright in the first place.

LEGAL CASES: OPEN EDUCATION

In the sixteen years since our licenses were first published, the number of lawsuits turning on the interpretation of a CC license has been extremely low, especially considering that more than 1.6 billion CC-licensed works are available on the Internet. CC licenses have fared incredibly well in court, and disputes are rare when compared to the number of lawsuits between the parties to privately negotiated, custom licenses.[1]

In 2017–18 there were three legal cases that involved CC licenses: *Great Minds vs. FedEx Office*, *Great Minds vs. Office Depot*, and *Philpot vs. Media Research Center*. The outcomes of the court decisions for these three cases favored the enforceability of CC licenses and their role in enabling the sharing of content with the public.

Great Minds vs. FedEx Office and Great Minds vs. Office Depot

Two of the three cases were raised by Great Minds, a curriculum developer.[2] In these two cases, Great Minds received public funding from New York State to develop OER (open educational resources) for school districts, which the organization licensed under CC BY-NC-SA 4.0. Great Minds brought the court cases against commercial copy shops that were hired by school districts to reproduce NC-licensed OER. The OER were for school use, which qualified as a noncommercial purpose.

Great Minds made a common assertion in both cases: school districts are not allowed to outsource the reproduction of educational materials licensed under CC BY-NC-SA 4.0 to contractors (the contractors were the commercial print shops in these cases) that make a profit on those reproductions. Great Minds' theory was that it was lawful for a school district employee to go to a copy shop and pay to use their copiers; however, if the same school employee paid the copy shop to hit "PRINT" instead, the copy shop is no longer working on behalf of, or under the direction of the school district—but is instead acting independently; therefore, the copy shop has to directly rely on *its own* NC license to make and charge a fee for the very same copies.

Because they had applied a noncommercial license to their OER, Great Minds claimed that the school districts working with the OER were not allowed to engage FedEx or Office Depot to reproduce the materials, and that because the copy shops had made a profit, they had violated the license. Importantly, Great Minds never alleged that the school districts' use of the reproduced materials violated the noncommercial restriction of the license.

The central question in both cases was whether a licensee (a school district that is properly using the work for noncommercial purposes) may outsource the reproduction of the works to another entity that makes a profit on those reproductions, without the entity it pays becoming a copyright infringer under the NC license.

In both cases, the district courts agreed with the copy shop and found that no copyright infringement or violation of the CC license had occurred. For additional details on the court cases, see the *Additional Resources* section at the end of this chapter.

Philpot vs. Media Research Center

The third case, *Philpot vs. Media Research Center, Inc.*,[3] involved Larry Philpot, who voluntarily shared two photographs on Wikimedia under a Creative Commons license. Philpot complained that Media Research Center (MRC) had infringed his copyrights when it published his photographs in articles *without* attribution.

Following discovery (the phase of litigation during which factual evidence is gathered), MRC filed a motion for a summary judgment asking the court to find that it had not infringed Philpot's copyrights because it used the photos for purposes of news and commentary, and those uses constitute fair use under U.S. copyright law.

In its decision granting the motion for summary judgment, the U.S. District Court for the Eastern District of Virginia rejected Philpot's argument that a "meeting of the minds" had to occur before the CC license used by Philpot applied.

The district court ultimately found that MRC's uses of the two photographs constituted fair use under U.S. copyright law, and as a result MRC had not violated Philpot's copyrights. The court concluded that because fair use applied, attribution under the CC license was not required, and so MRC had not infringed Philpot's copyrights. Compliance with the license had not been violated because a copyright license does not apply where fair use applies.

Fair use eliminates the need to rely on or comply with a CC license. This is the core design of all CC licenses—CC licenses grant permission when permission is required under copyright law. They communicate the licensor's intention to grant permission where permission is needed. And CC licenses are designed to be effective and enforceable without necessarily meeting the requirements of a contract. The law of contracts or obligations varies around the world, and there are some legal systems that may treat CC licenses as enforceable under the law of obligations. This court correctly determined that under U.S. law the licenses effectively grant permission without needing to meet the formal requirements of a contract because the intention to grant permission is all that is needed.

Final Remarks

Sharing your content using Creative Commons licenses is generous, but that alone is not enough to make it easy for others to reuse and remix your work. You should spend some time thinking from the perspective of someone who finds your shared content. How easy is it for them to download, reuse, and revise it? Are there legal or technical obstacles that make it difficult for them to do the things the CC license is designed to allow?

4.3 | FINDING AND REUSING CC-LICENSED WORKS

The "knowledge commons" of CC-licensed and public domain works is a plentiful resource that is available to all of us. But when you draw from it, remember to give credit to the creator and follow the other relevant license terms.

LEARNING OUTCOMES
- Search for and discover CC-licensed works
- Give proper attribution when reusing CC-licensed works

THE BIG QUESTION: WHY IT MATTERS

There are more than a billion CC-licensed works on the web. How do you find what might be useful to you? And once you do, what do you need to do when you reuse it?

There are several different ways to go about discovering CC-licensed works. Search engines can help you search across the web, or you can target particular platforms or sites. When you find a work to reuse, the most important thing to do is provide proper attribution to the work's licensor.

PERSONAL REFLECTION: WHY IT MATTERS TO YOU

Think about a few of the CC-licensed works you have seen or interacted with. How did you find them? Did you know how to attribute the author if you shared the work?

Acquiring Essential Knowledge

When you are seeking CC-licensed works to reuse, there are several strategies to consider. One good starting point is CC Search (https://search.creative

commons.org/), which is a tool that lets you search twelve major repositories of CC content online. Creative Commons is currently working on a project to improve the search tools it offers to help people discover works in the commons. Check out the prototype of a new version of CC Search at (https://ccsearch.creativecommons.org/), which lets you create and save lists of works you like and includes a tool that enables you to give attribution with a single click.

These search tools only scratch the surface of what is in the commons. Many platforms that enable the CC licensing of works shared on their sites also have their own search filters to find CC content, like OER Commons.

If there is a particular type of content you're looking for, you may be able to narrow down particular sources to explore. *Wikipedia* offers a fairly comprehensive listing (licensed CC BY-SA 3.0) of many major sources of CC material across various domains at https://en.wikipedia.org/wiki/List_of_major _Creative_Commons_licensed_works.

You can also search for works under a particular CC license. Take a look at the Creative Commons overview of each license that includes examples of projects and people using those licenses:

- You can find examples of use organized by CC license at https://creative commons.org/share-your-work/licensing-types-examples/licensing -examples/.
- You can find examples of works placed into the public domain using CC0 at https://creativecommons.org/share-your-work/public-domain/cc0/.

REUSING CC CONTENT

When you find a CC work you want to reuse, the single most important thing to know is how to provide attribution. *All CC licenses require that attribution be given to the creator.* (Remember that unlike the CC licenses, CC0 is not a license but a Public Domain Dedication tool, so it does not require attribution in its terms. Nevertheless, giving credit or citing the source is typically considered best practice even when not legally required.)

The elements of attribution are simple, though generally speaking, the more information you can provide, the better. People like to understand where CC-licensed works come from, and creators like to know that their names will remain attached to their works. If an author has provided extensive information in their attribution notice, you should retain it where possible.

As mentioned in section 4.1, the best practice for attribution is applying the TASL approach.

> T = Title
> A = Author
> S = Source
> L = License

The attribution requirements in the CC licenses are purposely designed to be fairly flexible in order to account for the many ways content is used. A filmmaker will have different options for giving credit than a scientist publishing an academic paper. Explore the CC wiki page "Best Practices for Attribution" (licensed CC BY 4.0 and available at https://wiki.creativecommons.org/wiki/Best_practices_for_attribution). Among the options listed, think about how you would prefer to be attributed for your own work.

Creative Commons is also exploring ways to automate attribution. Explore this feature by going to the CC search tool (https://ccsearch.creativecommons.org) and searching for "golden retrievers." Then, click on a couple of different photos to see how attribution is given, and experiment with the "copy credit as text" and "copy credit as HTML" functions.

The other main consideration when copying works (as opposed to remixing, which will be covered in the next section of this chapter) is the NonCommercial restriction. If the work you are using is published with one of the three CC licenses that includes the NC element, then you need to make sure that you're not using it for a commercial purpose.

Remember, you can always reach out to the creator if you want to request extra permission beyond what the license allows.

Final Remarks

Attribution is arguably the single most important aspect of Creative Commons licensing. Think about why you want credit for your own work, even when it may not be legally required. What value does attribution provide to authors, and to the public who comes across the work online?

4.4 | REMIXING CC-LICENSED WORKS

Combining and adapting CC-licensed works is where things can get a little tricky. This section will give you the tools you need.

LEARNING OUTCOMES
- Describe the basics of what it means to create an adaptation
- Explain the scope of the ShareAlike clause
- Explain the scope of the NoDerivatives clause
- Identify what *license compatibility* means and how to determine whether licenses are compatible

THE BIG QUESTION: WHY IT MATTERS
The great promise of Creative Commons licensing is that it increases the pool of content from which we can draw to create new works. But to take advantage of this potential, you have to understand when and how you can incorporate and adapt CC-licensed works. This requires careful attention to the particular CC licenses that apply, as well as a working understanding of the legal concept of adaptations as a matter of copyright.

Personal Reflection: Why It Matters to You

Have you ever wondered how to use a CC-licensed work created by someone else in something you are creating? Have you ever come across a CC-licensed work you wanted to reuse, but were unsure about whether doing so would require you to apply a ShareAlike license to what you created?

Acquiring Essential Knowledge

Copying a CC-licensed work and sharing it is pretty simple. Just make sure to provide attribution and refrain from using the work for commercial purposes if it is licensed with one of the NonCommercial licenses.

But what if you are changing a CC-licensed work or incorporating it into a new work? First, remember that if your use of someone else's CC-licensed work falls under an exception or limitation to copyright (like fair use or fair dealing), then you have no obligations under the CC license. But if that is not the case, then you need to rely on the CC license for permission to adapt the work. *The threshold question then becomes, is what you are doing creating an adaptation?*

An "adaptation" (or a "derivative work," as it is called in some parts of the world) is a special term in copyright law.[4] It means a "modified" or "transformed" work that has been created from a copyrighted work and that is sufficiently original to itself to be protected by copyright. (It can thus be regarded as a "new" work.) Whether a transformed work differs sufficiently from the original work to be called an "adaptation" is not always easy to determine, though some bright lines do exist. Read the explanation on the Creative Commons site at https://creativecommons.org/faq/#what-is-an-adaptation about what constitutes an adaptation. Some examples of adaptations include a film based on a novel and a translation of a book from one language into another.

Keep in mind that not all changes to a work result in the creation of an adaptation—such as spelling corrections. Also remember that to constitute an adaptation, the resulting work must be considered *based on* or *derived from* the original. This means that if you use a few lines from a poem to illustrate a poetry technique in an article you're writing, your article is not an adaptation because your article is not derived from or based on the poem from which you took a few lines. However, if you rearranged the stanzas in the poem and added new lines, then almost certainly the resulting work would be considered an adaptation.

Here are some particular types of adaptations to consider (some of them should be familiar from earlier sections of this book):

- Taking excerpts of a larger work. Read the relevant FAQ at https:// creativecommons.org/faq/#can-i-reuse-an-excerpt-of-a-larger-work -that-is-licensed-with-the-noderivs-restriction.
- Using a work in a different format. Read the relevant FAQ at https:// creativecommons.org/faq/#can-i-take-a-cc-licensed-work-and-use-it -in-a-different-format.
- Modifying a work. Read the relevant FAQ at https://creativecommons .org/faq/#when-is-my-use-considered-an-adaptation.

Fundamental principle

As of Version 4.0, all CC licenses, even the NoDerivatives licenses, allow anyone to make an adaptation of a CC-licensed work. The difference between ND licenses and the other licenses is that if an adaptation of an ND-licensed work has been created, it cannot be shared with others. So an individual can create adaptations of an ND-licensed work, but he/she is not allowed to share these with others, including the learners at an educational institution.

If your reuse of a CC-licensed work does not create an adaptation, then

- you are not required to apply a ShareAlike-license to your overall work if you are using an SA-licensed work within it;
- the ND restriction does not prevent you from using an ND-licensed work; and
- you can combine that CC-licensed material with other work as long as you attribute and comply with the NonCommercial restriction if it applies.

If your reuse of a CC-licensed work does create an adaptation, then there are limits on whether and how you may share the adapted work. We will look at those next. But first, a note about collections of materials.

ADAPTATIONS AND REMIXES VS. COLLECTIONS

Introductory note: The distinction between adaptations and collections is one of the trickiest concepts in copyright law. While there are many situations in which the differences are clear, there are also several ambiguous scenarios. The distinction between adaptations and remixes is even less clear; it varies by jurisdiction, and even within a given jurisdiction, a judge's determination between the two can be subjective, since there are few definitive rules on which to rely.

In contrast to an adaptation or remix, a collection involves the assembly of separate and independent creative works into a collective whole. *A collection is **not** an adaptation.* One community member likened the difference between adaptations and collections to smoothies and TV dinners, respectively:

1. Like a smoothie (figure 4.9), an *adaptation or remix* mixes material from different sources to create a wholly new work.

    In an adaptation or remix (and a smoothie), you often cannot tell where one constituent work ends and another one begins. While this flexibility is useful for the new creator, it is still important to provide attribution to the individual parts that went into making the adaptation.

    An example of an educational adaptation would be an open textbook chapter that weaves together multiple OER in such a way that the reader can't tell which resource was used on which page. That said, the endnotes of the book chapter should still provide attribution to all of the sources that were remixed in the chapter.

FIGURE 4.9 **CC Smoothie**

Author: Nate Angell | CC BY
Derivative of "Strawberry Smoothie on Glass Jar" by Element5 (pexels.com/photo/strawberry-smoothie-on-glass-jar-775032/) in the public domain, and various Creative Commons license icons by Creative Commons (https://creativecommons.org/about/downloads) used under CC BY.
Desaturated from original

2. Like a TV dinner (figure 4.10), a *collection* groups different works together; however, a collection keeps them organized as distinct and separate objects. An example of a collection would be a book that consists of a group of essays from different sources, or by different authors.

   When you create a collection, you must provide attribution and licensing information about each of the individual works in that collection. This gives the public the information they need to understand who created what and which license terms apply to specific content. You can revisit section 4.1 "Choosing and Applying a CC License" to learn how to properly indicate the copyright status of third-party works that you incorporate into your new work.

   When you combine material into a collection, you may have a *separate* copyright of your own that you may license. However, your copyright

FIGURE 4.10 **CC TV Dinner**

Author: Nate Angell | CC BY
Derivative of "tv dinner 1" by adrigu (https://flic.kr/p/6AMLDF) under CC BY, and various Creative Commons license icons by Creative Commons (https://creativecommons.org/about/downloads) used under CC BY.
Desaturated from original

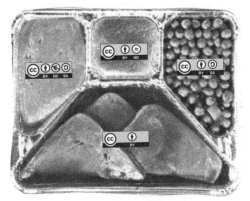

only extends to the new contributions that you made to the work. In a collection, this is the selection and arrangement of the various works in the collection, and not the individual works themselves. For example, you can select and arrange pre-existing poems published by others into an anthology, write an introduction, and design a cover for the collection, but your copyright and the only copyright you can license extends to your arrangement of the poems (not the poems themselves), and your original introduction and cover. The poems are not yours to license.

WHAT HAPPENS WHEN YOU CREATE AN ADAPTATION OF A CC-LICENSED WORK OR WORKS?

General rules

- If the underlying work is licensed under a NoDerivatives license, you can make and use changes privately, but you cannot share your adaptation with others, as discussed above.
- If the underlying or original work is licensed under a ShareAlike license, then ShareAlike applies to your adaptation of it, and you must license the adaptation under the same or a compatible license. There is more on this below.
- You need to consider license compatibility. *License compatibility* is the term used to address the issue of which types of licensed works can be adapted into a new work.
- In all cases, you have to attribute the original work when you create an adaptation.

Scenarios

When creating an adaptation of a CC-licensed work, the simplest scenario is when you take a single CC-licensed work and adapt it.

The more complicated scenario is when you are adapting two or more CC-licensed works into a new work.

In both situations, you need to consider what options you have for licensing the copyright you have in your adaptation; this is called the *Adapter's License*. Remember that your rights in your adaptation only apply to your own contributions. The original license continues to govern the reuse of the elements from the original work that you used when creating your adaptation. The "CC Adapters License Chart," shown in figure 4.11, may be a helpful guide. When creating an adaptation of material under the license identified in the left-hand column, you may license your contributions to the adaptation under one of the licenses indicated on the top row if the corresponding box is dark gray. Creative Com-

Adapter's license chart		Adapter's license						
		BY	BY-NC	BY-NC-ND	BY-NC-SA	BY-ND	BY-SA	PD
Status of original work	PD							
	BY							
	BY-NC							
	BY-NC-ND							
	BY-NC-SA							
	BY-ND							
	BY-SA							

FIGURE 4.11 **CC adapter's license chart**

*Figure from Creative Commons: https://creativecommons.org/faq/#can-i-combine-material
 -under-different-creative-commons-licenses-in-my-work
CC BY 4.0 | Desaturated from original*

mons does not recommend using a license if the corresponding box is white, although doing so is technically permitted by the terms of the license. If you do, you should take additional care to mark the adaptation as involving multiple copyrights under different terms, so that downstream users are aware of their obligations to comply with the licenses from all rights holders. The light gray boxes indicate those licenses that you may not use as your adapter's license.

HOW TO PICK YOUR ADAPTER'S LICENSE

If the underlying work is licensed with BY or BY-NC, we recommend that your adapter's license include at least the same license elements as the license applied to the original. For example, if one adapts a BY-NC work, she will apply BY-NC to her adaptation. If one adapts a BY work, she could apply either BY or BY-NC to her adaptation.

If the underlying work is licensed with BY-SA or BY-NC-SA, your adapter's license must be the same license applied to the original or a license that is desig-nated as compatible to the original license. We'll discuss license compatibility in more detail below.

Remember, if the underlying work is licensed with BY-ND or BY-NC-ND, you cannot distribute adaptations, so you don't need to be concerned about what adapter's license to apply.

UNDERSTANDING LICENSE COMPATIBILITY

When people talk about licenses being "compatible," they can be referring to several different situations.

One type of license compatibility involves the question of what licenses you can use for your adapter's license when you adapt a work. This is what we discussed above. For example, BY-NC is compatible with BY, in the sense that one can adapt a BY work and use BY-NC on her adaptation.

By definition, the ShareAlike licenses have very few compatible licenses. All SA licenses after Version 1.0 allow you to use a later version of the same license on your adaptation. For example, if you remix a BY-SA 2.0 work, you can, and should, apply BY-SA 4.0 to your adaptation. There are also a small number of non-CC licenses that have been designated as CC Compatible Licenses for Share-Alike purposes. You can read more about this at https://creativecommons.org/share-your-work/licensing-considerations/compatible-licenses.

Another type of license compatibility relates to what licenses are compatible when adapting (more commonly referred to as "remixing" in this context) more than one pre-existing work. The remix chart in figure 4.12 may be a helpful guide in these circumstances. To use the chart, find a license that applies to one of the works on the left-hand column and the license that applies to the other

	PUBLIC DOMAIN	PUBLIC DOMAIN	BY	BY SA	BY NC	BY ND	BY NC SA	BY NC ND
PUBLIC DOMAIN	✓	✓	✓	✓	✓	✗	✓	✗
PUBLIC DOMAIN	✓	✓	✓	✓	✓	✗	✓	✗
BY	✓	✓	✓	✓	✓	✗	✓	✗
BY SA	✓	✓	✓	✓	✗	✗	✗	✗
BY NC	✓	✓	✓	✗	✓	✗	✓	✗
BY ND	✗	✗	✗	✗	✗	✗	✗	✗
BY NC SA	✓	✓	✓	✗	✓	✗	✓	✗
BY NC ND	✗	✗	✗	✗	✗	✗	✗	✗

FIGURE 4.12 **CC License Compatibility Chart**

Figure from Creative Commons: https://creativecommons.org/faq/#can-i-combine-material -under-different-creative-commons-licenses-in-my-work
CC BY 4.0 | Destaurated from original

work on the top right row. If there is a checkmark in the box where that row and column intersect, then the works under those two licenses can be remixed. If there is an "X" in the box, then the works may not be remixed unless an exception or limitation applies.

When using the chart, you can determine which license to use for your adaptation by choosing the more restrictive of the two licenses on the works you're combining. While this technically isn't your only option for your adapter's license, it is best practice because it eases reuse for downstream users.

Final Remarks

It can be intimidating to approach remixing in a way that is consistent with copyright. In this section, hopefully you gained some tools for how to approach the task. The threshold question is whether an adaptation under copyright is created. Once that is answered, you have the information you need to determine what works from the commons you can incorporate into your work.

4.5 | ADDITIONAL RESOURCES

Additional Details on the Court Cases in Section 4.2 "Things to Consider after CC Licensing"

In the *FedEx Office* case, the decision was affirmed by the U.S. 2nd Circuit Court of Appeals, which stated: "In sum, the unambiguous terms of License permit FedEx to copy the Materials on behalf of a school district exercising rights under the License and charge that district for that copying at a rate more than FedEx's cost, in the absence of any claim that the school district is using the Materials for other than a 'non-Commercial purpose.' The motion to dismiss is granted."

With the *Office Depot* case, Great Minds claimed that the copy store had violated the BY-NC-SA 4.0 license for the same reasons FedEx Office did; however, Great Minds also claimed that because Office Depot had reached out to school districts to solicit reproduction orders, the solicitation was additional evidence of a license violation. The other difference with the *FedEx Office* case was that Great Minds and Office Depot had entered into a contract specifying that Office Depot could reproduce the same publicly funded educational materials for school districts and would pay royalties to Great Minds.[5]

The U.S. District Court for the Central District of California agreed with Office Depot, stating that it "concludes that the Creative Commons Public License unambiguously grants the licensee schools and school districts the right 'to reproduce and Share the Licensed Material, in whole or in part, for NonCommercial purposes only,' and does not prohibit the schools and school districts from employing third parties, such as Office Depot, to make copies of the Materials. . . . Because the schools and school districts are the entities exercising the rights granted under the Creative Commons Public License, it is irrelevant that Office Depot may have profited from making copies for schools and school districts."

Furthermore, the district court stated: "The Creative Commons Public License at issue authorizes schools to: (1) reproduce and use the Materials for NonCommercial purposes, (2) expressly permits the schools to provide those Materials to the public 'by any means or process,' and (3) does not prohibit the schools from outsourcing the copying to third-party vendors. Because a licensee may lawfully use a third-party agent or contractor to assist it in exercising its licensed rights, absent contractual provisions prohibiting such activity, Great Minds has failed to allege that Office Depot's conduct was outside the scope of the license and, thus, Great Minds' claim for copyright infringement against Office Depot fails." The court also addressed Office Depot's alleged solicitation of school districts' reproduction business. The court did not find the difference urged by Great Minds persuasive or that it should change the outcome. The *Office Depot* case remains pending on appeal before the U.S. 9th Circuit Court of Appeals as of August 15, 2019. Oral argument appears likely in November 2019, and a decision will follow.

More Information about Modifying the Licenses

The following two entries are selected "Frequently Asked Questions," by Creative Commons. CC BY 4.0.

- "Can I change the license terms and conditions?" https://creativecommons. org/faq/#can-i-change-the-license-terms-or-conditions.

- "Can I enter into separate or supplemental agreements with users of my work?" https://creativecommons.org/faq/#can-i-enter-into-separate-or-supplemental-agreements-with-users-of-my-work.

- "Modifying the CC Licenses," by Creative Commons. CC BY 4.0.
    This provides Creative Commons policy guidance for modifying the CC licenses: https://wiki.creativecommons.org/wiki/Modifying_the _CC_licenses.

More Information about Marking Licensed Works

- "Marking/Creators/Marking Third Party Content," by Creative Commons. CC BY 4.0.
  This wiki provides best practices and nuanced information on the marking of third-party content: https://wiki.creativecommons.org/wiki/Marking/Creators/Marking_third_party_content#Additional _explanation_and_tips.

More Information about License Compatibility

- "Compatible Licenses," by Creative Commons. CC BY 4.0.
  This is a page with information on which licenses are compatible, how compatibility works, and where there may not necessarily be compatibility between licenses: https://creativecommons.org/share-your -work/licensing-considerations/compatible-licenses.

- "Wiki/CC License Compatibility," by Creative Commons. CC BY 4.0.
  This page gives more information on the CC license compatibility chart: https://wiki.creativecommons.org/wiki/Wiki/cc_license _compatibility.

- "License Compatibility," *Wikipedia* article. CC BY-SA 3.0.
  This is *Wikipedia*'s article on license compatibility, including open licenses that are not CC licenses: https://en.wikipedia.org/wiki/ License_compatibility.

More Scholarship about CC Licenses

- "Creative Commons Licenses Legal Pitfalls: Incompatibilities and Solutions," by Melanie Dulong de Rosnay at the Institute for Information Law at the University of Amsterdam and Creative Commons Netherlands. CC BY 3.0 NL.
  This is a detailed report on the more nuanced and legal aspects of incompatibilities which apply in a variety of international applications: https://www.creativecommons.nl/downloads/101220 cc_incompatibilityfinal.pdf.

- "User-Related Drawbacks of Open Content Licensing," by Till Kreutzer in *Open Content Licensing: From Theory to Practice*, edited by Lucie Guibault and Christina Angelopoulos (Amsterdam: Amsterdam University Press, 2011). CC BY NC 3.0

This is a book chapter about some complicated issues that pertain to the users of openly licensed materials (including CC licenses).

Participants' Recommended Resources

CC Certificate participants have recommended many additional resources through Hypothes.is annotations on the Certificate website. While Creative Commons has not vetted these resources, we wanted to highlight the participants' suggestions here: https://certificates.creativecommons.org/cccertedu comments/chapter/additional-resources-4/.

NOTES

1. One of Creative Commons' roles is to serve as a responsible public license steward, actively providing guidance and education about its licenses. When Creative Commons considers weighing in on disputes with commentary or the filing of friend-of-the-court briefs, CC always acts as an advocate for the licenses and their proper interpretation, never in favor of or against a particular litigant. For a detailed analysis of Creative Commons case law, see section 3.4 "License Enforceability." Creative Commons maintains a database of court decisions and case law from jurisdictions around the world on the Creative Commons wiki for Case Law (licensed CC BY 4.0, available at https://wiki.creativecommons.org/wiki/Case_Law).

2. The official names of the court cases are: "Great Minds v. FedEx Office and Print Services, Inc., U.S. District Court for the Eastern District of New York (Civil Action 2:16-cv-01462-DRH-ARL)" and "Great Minds vs. Office Depot, Inc., U.S. District Court for the Central District of California (CV 17-7435-JFW)."

3. The official name of the court case is "Larry Philpot v Media Research Center Inc., U.S. District Court for the Eastern District of Virginia, Case 1:17-cv-822."

4. You learned about the terms adaptation and derivative work in chapter 2, and how CC licenses use those terms.

5. According to the complaint, this contract was entered into while FedEx Office was pending. However, once the district court granted the motion to dismiss in favor of FedEx Office, Office Depot terminated its contract with Great Minds shortly before it expired and, in reliance on the FedEx Office decision, continued to reproduce Great Minds' materials for school districts without paying royalties to Great Minds.

Creative Commons for Librarians and Educators

AS THE ROLE OF LIBRARIES EVOLVES AND EXPANDS IN OUR FAST-CHANGING information environment, expertise in open licensing has become a crucial asset for the modern librarian.

Creative Commons powers the open education movement with tools that help create better, more flexible, and more sustainable open educational resources (OER), practices, and policies. Creative Commons licenses are the most popular open licenses in open education and Open Access (OA) projects around the world; CC puts the "open" in OER and OA. This chapter will introduce you to the specifics of using CC licenses and CC-licensed content for educational and research purposes.

This chapter has seven sections:

1. Open Access to Scholarship
2. Open Pedagogy and Practices
3. OER, Open Textbooks, Open Courses
4. Finding, Evaluating, and Adapting Resources
5. Creating and Sharing OER
6. Opening Up Your Institution
7. Additional Resources

Before you start this chapter, you should consider joining the Creative Commons Open Education Platform at https://creativecommons.org/2017/09/05/invitation-join-cc-open-education-platform. Your input can help us identify, plan, and coordinate multinational open education content, practices, and policy projects in order to collaboratively solve education challenges around the world. Be sure to briefly tell us (1) why you'd like to join and (2) who you are—this helps CC avoid accepting "spammers."

5.1 | OPEN ACCESS TO SCHOLARSHIP

What is Open Access scholarly literature? Open Access literature is digital, online, free of charge, and free of most copyright and licensing restrictions. Open Access stands in contrast to the existing "closed" system for communicating scientific and scholarly research. This system is slow, expensive, and ill-suited for research collaboration and discovery. And even though scholarly research is largely produced as a result of public funding, the results are often hidden behind technical, legal, and financial barriers or paywalls. Open Access publishing is an alternative model—one that takes full advantage of digital technologies, the web, and open licensing to provide free access to scholarship.

LEARNING OUTCOMES
- Define Open Access
- Explain the benefits of Open Access for your learners and for researchers at your institution
- Understand how authors and researchers can make their own works Open Access

THE BIG QUESTION: WHY IT MATTERS
The purpose of scientific inquiry at a university is the fundamental search for knowledge. Teaching, the open exchange of ideas, and the process of publishing original research are all methods by which academic faculty, learners, staff, and others contribute to advancing scholarship.

How well do the current practices of accessing and sharing information within the university system reflect and support the stated goals of research and scholarship?

This chapter will explore how the practice of Open Access publishing aligns with the goals of improving access to knowledge, and how librarians can support colleges and universities in implementing Open Access practices and policies.

PERSONAL REFLECTION: WHY IT MATTERS TO YOU

How does your institution support (or not support) the open publication of research? How do you interact with learners and faculty who are searching for academic research? Have you ever encountered a paywall while trying to access research articles?

Acquiring Essential Knowledge

SCHOLARLY PUBLISHING TODAY

To get an overview of the topic, you should first read the *Wikipedia* article on "Scholarly Communication" (licensed CC BY-SA 3.0 and available at https://en.wikipedia.org/wiki/Scholarly_communication). This article defines scholarly communication as "the system through which research and other scholarly writings are created, evaluated for quality, disseminated to the scholarly community, and preserved for future use. The system includes both formal means of communication, such as publication in peer-reviewed journals, and informal channels, such as electronic listservs."

The challenges with the existing approach to scholarly communications are laid out in the graphic in figure 5.1. This image explains—in generalized terms—the current process involved with developing and communicating scientific results. In the first step of the life cycle, scientists, academics, and research

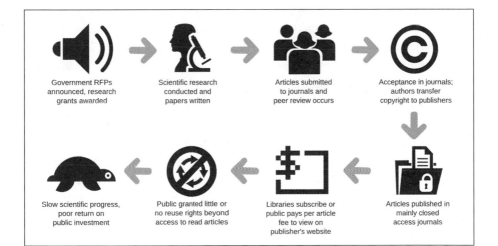

FIGURE 5.1 **Current funding cycle for research articles**

Figure from Creative Commons Wiki: https://wiki.creativecommons.org/wiki/File:Research
_articles_cycles.jpg
Author: Billymeinke | CC BY 4.0 | Cropped and desaturated from original

institutions seek funds to conduct a variety of research. Most often this funding comes from government sources (e.g., the National Institutes of Health in the United States), although there are several philanthropic foundations (such as the Bill & Melinda Gates Foundation) that are now making major investments in particular types of research.

After the researchers have secured their grants, they conduct their experiments and collect their data. Most of the time these researchers prepare their results in the form of an academic article, which they then submit to a scholarly journal for publication. The journals then arrange for some of the submitted articles to undergo a process of peer review, in which experts within that particular topic or field will read, review, and usually provide comments on the submitted paper.

Some of the articles that pass the peer review stage are then offered for publication in the journal. The journal will notify the author that her paper has been accepted, and usually require that the author transfer copyright in the article to (or agree to an exclusive publishing contract with) the journal. By accepting these terms, the author has granted to the journal her exclusive rights under copyright. This means that the journal—and not the author—is now the copyright holder of the article, and so the *journal* may restrict the terms of access and reuse provided for by the bundle of rights granted to rights holders under the law.

Because journals have become the de facto rights holders to the articles in which new scientific research is published, they are also in a position to license access to these materials to university libraries, research institutions, and the public—typically for a significant fee. This leads to a cyclical situation in which for-profit publishers essentially sell back access to the scientific and scholarly record that academics originally produced through public grants.

Even after a publishing embargo (usually a time of six months to a year, during which the publishers retain exclusive publishing rights) expires, access to the mostly publicly funded scientific research remains limited, with users only permitted to read those articles if they are properly submitted to institutional repositories. In the end, the public is left with restricted access to the publicly funded scholarly record, and progress in the scientific enterprise doesn't reach its maximum potential.

There are several critiques of the existing academic publishing system. SPARC has a summary of their key points on its "Open Access" page (licensed

CC BY 4.0, available at https://sparcopen.org/open-access/), some highlights of which are given below:

- Governments provide most of the funding for research—many billions of dollars annually—and public institutions employ a large portion of all researchers.
- Researchers publish their findings without the expectation of compensation. Unlike other authors, they hand their work over to publishers without payment, in the interest of advancing human knowledge.
- Through the process of peer review, researchers review each other's work for free.
- Once published, those that contributed to the research (from taxpayers to the institutions that supported the research itself) have to pay again to access the findings. Though research is produced as a public good, it isn't available to the public who paid for it. (2007-2017 SPARC, CC BY)

As ever-increasing journal prices outpace library budgets, academic libraries are forced to make difficult decisions—often having to cancel subscriptions or shift money away from other budget items. According to the Association of Research Libraries (ARL), the average cost of a serial subscription for ARL member libraries increased by 315 percent from 1986 to 2003.[1] Since 2003, average journal prices have increased more slowly, but they've still continued to rise about nine percent each year.

OPEN ACCESS PUBLISHING
The "closed access" publishing system limits the impact of the research produced by the scientific and scholarly community and progress is thereby slowed significantly. By contrast, Open Access literature is defined by the scholar Peter Suber as "digital, online, free of charge, and free of most copyright and licensing restrictions."[2] The graphic in figure 5.2 provides a quick overview of how an open-access publishing system works.

In contrast to figure 5.1, which explained the current costly and inefficient science publishing life cycle, figure 5.2 explores an alternate path—the open access route.

The process begins just as it did in the explanation of the incumbent system—with government requests for proposals (RFPs) for research. But instead of remaining silent on how the research results will be communicated, the RFPs

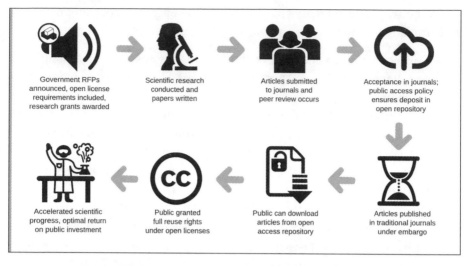

FIGURE 5.2 **Optimized funding cycle for research articles**

Figure from Creative Commons Wiki: https://wiki.creativecommons.org/wiki/File:Research
  _articles_cycles.jpg
Author: Billymeinke | CC BY 4.0 | Cropped and desaturated from original

contain policy language which requires that the published research be made available on an open access basis.

Next, researchers conduct their scientific experiments and prepare their academic manuscripts. When they go to submit their articles to journals, they must think about the Open-Access policy requirements they agreed upon when they accepted their grant funding. This means that the researchers must retain their copyrights—and not sign them over to for-profit publishers. Or instead, authors must search out a "Gold" open access journal, which publishes research under liberal open-access licenses (like CC BY) at publication. In either case, authors retain some—or all—rights to their research articles, permitting them to publish under open access licenses, and ensuring that they may deposit their articles in a university or institutional repository for long-term access and preservation.

By publishing under open access licenses like CC BY, downstream users are granted the legal permissions to access and reuse the research. This type of

 Watch the *Open Access Explained!* video. **https://www.youtube.com/
watch?v=L5rVH1KGBCY&t=124s** | CC BY 3.0

open access system is better aligned with the original purpose of conducting science and sharing results openly through the scholarly publishing process. In the long run, the open access approach is more efficient, equitable, affordable, and collaborative.

OPEN ACCESS OPTIONS

Open Access authors have the opportunity to publish in a few ways. The most common are known as "Green" and "Gold" Open Access.

Green OA involves making a version of the article or manuscript freely available in a repository. This is also known as self-archiving. An example of Green OA is a university research repository. OA repositories can be organized by discipline (e.g., arXiv for physics) or institution (e.g., Knowledge@UChicago for the University of Chicago).

Gold OA involves making the final version of the manuscript freely available immediately upon publication by the publisher, typically by publishing it in an Open Access journal and making the article available under an open license. Typically, Open Access journals charge an article processing charge (APC) when an author wishes to (1) publish an article online allowing for free public access and (2) retain the copyright to the article. APCs range from zero to several thousand dollars per article. You can read more about APCs on *Wikipedia*'s "Article Processing Charge" (licensed CC BY-SA 3.0 and available at *https://en.wikipedia.org/wiki/Article_processing_charge*). An example of a Gold OA journal is PLOS Biology, one of several scientific journals put out by the nonprofit publisher PLOS (Public Library of Science).

The Directory of Open Access Journals (DOAJ; https://doaj.org/) is a site that indexes open access journals, and HowOpenIsIt? (licensed CC BY 4.0, available at https://sparcopen.org/our-work/howopenisit/) is a handy tool for evaluating the relative "openness" of journals from fully open-access to closed-access.

Certain emerging models like preprints and hubs are rapidly emerging, and they can provide a new way of considering Open Access publishing outside of the constraints of publisher-mediated models.

Educating Authors about Their Publishing Rights

By understanding copyright and the various scholarly publishing options, librarians can help faculty members and graduate learners navigate the system as they publish research.

Often, scholarly publishers require authors to transfer their rights to publishing companies before their research will be published in an academic journal. Academic librarians and other library departments can support faculty and student authors by helping them understand what they give up when they transfer their copyrights to a publisher. For example, scholarly authors who transfer copyright could lose the ability to post their research on their own websites.

Several tools exist to help faculty and scholars understand their rights and publishing options, and to help them exercise those rights. The Termination of Transfer tool,[3] co-stewarded by the Authors Alliance and Creative Commons, gives authors who have previously entered into publishing agreements information about whether and how they can regain the publication rights that they previously assigned away so they can publish on new terms, including under a CC license if they choose. The Scholars Copyright Addendum Engine[4] can be used by faculty and other authors to amend publication agreements when they are submitting an article to a traditional publisher. The engine allows authors to choose among different options to reserve rights for themselves and generates an agreement that is then submitted with a traditional publication agreement to make that legally effective. Additionally, the Authors Alliance publishes myriad resources about these tools and open access, and PLOS offers resources and articles about the benefits of open access as well.

Academic librarians can also help scholars understand how different publishing options affect both the audience and the prestige of their work. The "impact factor" is a primary metric of the prominence of a journal or publication, measured by the number of times the average article in a particular journal has been cited (in other sources) in one year. Because impact factors are not necessarily a reliable metric of a journal's importance, some publishers like Nature Research, the publisher of the prestigious scientific journal *Nature*, are reconsidering the importance of impact factors for journals. Many Open Access scholars encourage systems like altmetrics to provide another way of thinking about impact beyond the traditional metrics. In 2017, *Science* released a study finding that on average, open access papers had a fifty percent higher research impact than strictly "paywalled" papers.[5] For more information, read Jon Tennant's 2016 article (https://f1000research.com/articles/5-632/v1) on the academic, societal, and economic advantages of open access.

Open Access Practices and Policies
at the University and Beyond

An open access policy is a formal policy adopted by an institution to support researchers in making their work openly available. These policies can refer to published peer-reviewed articles, conference papers, and peer-reviewed drafts or pre-printed publications that are deposited in an institutional repository or published under open-access terms in a journal. Open access policies generally define the guidelines for how researchers can disseminate their research in order to maximize access to them. The Registry of Open Access Repository Mandates and Policies (ROARMAP; https://roarmap.eprints.org) is a registry that charts the open access policies or mandates adopted by universities, research institutions, and research funders that require or request their researchers to provide open access to their peer-reviewed research article output by depositing it in an institutional repository, or publish their research under open-access terms in a journal.

According to Peter Suber, an open access advocate, mandate is not the best word "'for open-access policies,' . . . but neither is any other English word."[6] Without a mandate, institutions can consider faculty opt-in policies, whereby libraries or copyright offices focus on shifting the default publishing practice to open access.

UNIVERSITY POLICIES

Many universities have adopted open access policies that require university-affiliated researchers to grant to their institution a non-exclusive license to a scholarly article at the time of the creation of the work. This process heads off problems with publishers downstream, since the university retains a legal right to the work before copyright is transferred to a publisher. These policies have proliferated under the assumption that universities themselves should be able to access and preserve the research outputs of their faculty. To view an example, review the University of California Open Access Policy at https://osc.universityofcalifornia.edu/open-access-policy/. You can also view many other institutions' open-access policies on the ROARMAP site (https://roarmap.eprints.org), which has collected several hundred of these policies, including those of universities, colleges, research organizations, and other academic institutions.

For academic librarians who are interested in developing an open access policy for their university or institution, the Harvard Open Access Project has developed a toolkit, licensed CC BY 3.0 and available at https://cyber.harvard. edu/hoap/Good_practices_for_university_open-access_policies. Open Access policies usually originate from an institution's Office of Scholarly Communications, but librarians in a variety of roles (outreach, reference, etc.) can also help craft these policies.

PUBLIC POLICY

In addition to encouraging the development of open access policies at the university level, public policies can ensure that publicly funded research be made available under Open Access terms. This typically is accomplished through the inclusion of sharing requirements that are tied to receiving government or philanthropic grant funds. When funding cycles for research include deposit or open license requirements for publications, the resulting increased access and opportunities for reuse extend the value of that research funding. As an example, the U.S. National Institutes of Health (NIH) Public Access Policy requires that "all investigators funded by the NIH submit or have submitted for them to the National Library of Medicine's PubMed Central an electronic version of their final, peer-reviewed manuscripts upon acceptance for publication, to be made publicly available no later than twelve months after the official date of publication."[7]

The Fair Access to Science and Technology Research Act (FASTR) was introduced repeatedly in both houses of Congress in the period from 2012 to 2017, but it has yet to be approved. Should U.S. Congress approve FASTR, the bill would require federal agencies with annual extramural research budgets of $100 million or more to provide the public with online access to the research articles stemming from that funded research within six to twelve months after publication in a peer-reviewed journal. The passage of FASTR would ensure that articles based on publicly funded research are made freely available for all potential users to read, and it would ensure that those articles can be fully used in the digital environment, enabling the use of new computational analysis tools that promise to revolutionize the research process.

Open Access Myths Debunked

For faculty and learners alike, open access can seem like a scary new world, particularly since the pressure to publish has increased. There are many guides to debunking the myths of open access publishing, and reading these carefully to dispel any fear or misunderstanding is crucial in the current academic landscape.

- "Field Guide to Misunderstandings about Open Access," by Peter Suber, http://legacy.earlham.edu/~peters/fos/newsletter/04-02-09.htm#fieldguide
- University of Minnesota, "Myths about Open Access Publishing," https://www.lib.umn.edu/openaccess/myths-about-open-access
- "Persistent Myths about Open Access Scientific Publishing," by Mike Taylor, https://www.theguardian.com/science/blog/2012/apr/17/persistent-myths-open-access-scientific-publishing

Final Remarks

Universities play a major role in advancing scientific research, and academic publishing is a key mechanism for faculty to communicate their findings to colleagues and the public. As organizers of knowledge within institutions, librarians can work together with university researchers to promote access to information. They can do this by educating on the "how" and "why" of open access, answering questions about copyright, and providing guidance and recommendations to maximize the reach and impact of scholarly publishing in particular fields.

5.2 | OPEN PEDAGOGY AND PRACTICES

Openness in education brings the potential for co-creation and learning through active participation in how knowledge is produced.

LEARNING OUTCOMES

- Explain how copyright restricts pedagogy
- Define open pedagogy, open educational practices, and OER-enabled pedagogy, and describe how open licensing enables each of these
- List examples of open pedagogy in practice

THE BIG QUESTION: WHY IT MATTERS

Do you remember when smartphones were first released? They were full of infinite possibilities compared to earlier phones. Before smartphones, we could only call and text. But with smartphones, we can now take videos and pictures, play movies and music, surf the web and read e-mail, and call and text. It was difficult for long-time users of older phones to take advantage of all the capabilities offered by the new phones. They were too accustomed to the limitations of older phones. For months—and sometimes years—they used their smartphones only to call and text. (Maybe you know someone like this?)

Many educators have the same problem with open educational resources. They have spent so much time using education materials published under restrictive licenses that they struggle to take advantage of the new pedagogical capabilities offered by OER. These pedagogical capabilities are all about the teaching and learning practices and tools that empower learners and teachers to create and share knowledge openly and learn deeply.

Three Definitions

The Open Education movement is still discussing and debating what it means to think about teaching and learning practices in a more inclusive, diverse, and open manner. You can read a few examples of how various educators approach this topic on the Year of Open (licensed CC BY 4.0, available at https://www.year ofopen.org/april-open-perspective-what-is-open-pedagogy/). At least three fundamental terms have emerged from this discussion:

- *Open Educational Practices* (from Cronin's 2018 Open Edu Global presentation): the use, reuse, or creation of OER and collaborative, pedagogical practices employing social and participatory technologies for interaction, peer-learning, knowledge creation and sharing, and the empowerment of learners.
- *Open Pedagogy* (from DeRosa and Jhangiani's chapter in the 2017 book, *A Guide to Making Open Textbooks with Students*): an access-oriented commitment to learner-driven education and a process of designing architectures and using tools for learning that enable learners to shape the public knowledge commons of which they are a part. (There is more on this at Open Pedagogy Notebook, licensed CC BY 4.0 and available at http://openpedagogy.org/open-pedagogy.)
- *OER-Enabled Pedagogy* (from Wiley and Hilton's 2018 journal article "Defining OER-Enabled Pedagogy"): a set of teaching and learning practices that are only possible or practical when you have permission to engage in the 5R activities [i.e., retain, reuse, revise, remix, and redistribute].

Personal Reflection: Why It Matters to You

When you've used open educational resources in the past, have you taken advantage of the permissions offered by their open licenses, or did you use OER just like you used your previous, traditionally copyrighted materials? In other words, did you do anything with the OER that was impossible to do with traditionally copyrighted materials? Why or why not?

Acquiring Essential Knowledge

It's well-established that people learn through activities. And it's equally well-established that copyright restricts people from engaging in a range of activities. When juxtaposed like this, it becomes clear that copyright restricts pedagogy by contracting the universe of things that learners and teachers can do with education materials. If there are things that learners are not allowed to do, this means there are ways that learners are not allowed to learn. If there are things that teachers aren't allowed to do, this means there are ways that teachers aren't allowed to teach.

You can learn about how these restrictions on what teachers and learners can do impacts teaching and learning by reading the metaphor/blog post about driving airplanes on roads at https://opencontent.org/blog/archives/3761.

Examples of Open Educational Practices, Open Pedagogy, and OER-Enabled Pedagogy

One of the foundational ideas of open teaching and learning practices is the distinction between disposable and renewable assignments.

Do you remember doing homework for school that felt utterly pointless? A "disposable assignment" is an assignment that supports an individual student's learning but adds no other value to the world—the student spends hours working on it, the teacher spends time grading it, and the student gets it back and then throws it away. While disposable assignments may promote learning by an individual student, these assignments can be demoralizing for people who want to feel like their work matters beyond the immediate moment.

In contrast, "renewable assignments" are assignments that both support individual student learning and add value to the broader world. With renewable assignments, learners are asked to create and openly license valuable artifacts that, in addition to supporting their own learning, will be useful to other learners both inside and outside the classroom. Classic renewable assignments include, for example, collaborating with learners to write new case studies for textbooks, creating "explainer" videos, and modifying learning materials that will speak more directly to learners' local cultures and needs.

To explore additional examples of this pedagogical approach in action, check out the examples given by David Wiley in Project Management for Instructional Designers (licensed CC BY-NC-SA 4.0, available at http://pm4id.org/) and Robin DeRosa's Actualham website (http://robinderosa.net/uncategorized/my-open-textbook-pedagogy-and-practice/) of learners adapting existing materials to create new textbooks. In both of these cases, teachers had learners create their own textbooks, which then had Creative Commons licenses applied to them. Other examples of OER-enabled pedagogy in action include assignments by JB Murray (licensed CC BY-SA 3.0 on https://en.wikipedia.org/wiki/Wikipedia:WikiProject_Murder_Madness_and_Mayhem) and Amin Azzam (licensed CC BY-SA 3.0 on https://en.wikipedia.org/wiki/Wikipedia:WikiProject_Medicine/UCSF_Elective_2013) that had learners significantly improve articles that were in *Wikipedia*. When they completed these assignments, the learners had created open artifacts that were useful in both supporting their own learning and the learning of other learners and educators. In these examples, learners created assignments that allowed them to interact with the greater community and ensured that the assignments are renewable, not disposable, artifacts.

A couple of other interesting examples of renewable assignments are a remixed explainer video that a student made, entitled *Blogs and Wikis: a fictitious debate* (https://www.youtube.com/watch?v=AsFU3sAlPx4) and the DS106 assignment bank (http://assignments.ds106.us/) which is a hub for student-created, CC-licensed content. Additional examples are available on the Open Pedagogy Notebook website (licensed CC BY 4.0 and available at http://open pedagogy.org/examples).

Final Remarks

If you're just going to use your new smartphone the same way you used your old flip phone, there wasn't much point in getting a new phone. Likewise, when we use OER to support learning in exactly the same ways that we used the old "all rights reserved" materials, we may save learners money, but we miss out on the transformative power of open pedagogy. As you prepare to use OER in your teaching, think about the new things that are possible in the context of permission to engage in the 5R activities.

5.3 | OER, OPEN TEXTBOOKS, OPEN COURSES

Open Education is an idea, as well as a set of content, practices, policies, and communities which, when properly leveraged, can help everyone in the world access free, effective, open learning materials at either zero or marginal cost. We live in an age of information abundance where everyone, for the first time in human history, can potentially attain all the education they desire. The key to this transformational shift in learning is Open Educational Resources (OER).

OER are educational materials that are shared at no cost, with legal permissions for the public to freely use, share, and build upon their content.

OER are possible because:

- they are (mostly) born digital,[8] and digital resources can be stored, copied, and distributed for near zero cost;
- the Internet makes it simple for the public to share digital content; and
- Creative Commons licenses make it simple and legal to retain copyright and legally share educational resources with the world.

Because we can share effective education materials with the world for near zero cost,[9] many people argue that educators and governments which support public education have a moral and ethical obligation to do so. After all, education is fundamentally about sharing knowledge and ideas. Creative Commons believes that OER will replace much of the expensive, proprietary content that is currently used in academic courses. Shifting to this open model will generate more equitable economic opportunities and social benefits globally without sacrificing the quality of educational content.

THE BIG QUESTION: WHY IT MATTERS

Does it seem reasonable that education in the age of the Internet should be more expensive and less flexible than it was in previous generations? Education is more important than ever before; nothing else can do as much to promote the happiness, prosperity, and security of individuals, families, and societies. While many interesting and useful experiments are occurring outside formal education, the degrees, certificates, and other credentials awarded by formal institutions are still critically important to the quality of life of many people around the world.

Formal education, even in the age of the Internet, can be more expensive and less flexible than ever. In many countries, the publishers of educational materials overcharge for textbooks and other resources. As part of their transition from print to digital, these same companies have largely moved away from a model where learners purchase and own books to a "streaming" model where they have access to those resources for only a limited time. Furthermore, publishers are constantly developing new restrictive technologies that limit what learners and faculty can do with the resources they have temporary access to, including novel ways to prohibit printing, prevent cutting and pasting, and restrict the sharing of materials between friends.

LEARNING OUTCOMES
- Define the word open in the context of open educational resources
- Differentiate between OER, open textbooks, open courses, and MOOCs (massive open online courses)

PERSONAL REFLECTION: WHY IT MATTERS TO YOU
What impacts have the rising costs and decreased flexibility of educational materials had on you and those you know? What role do you think that "all rights reserved" copyrights and related laws have played in driving up costs and driving down flexibility for learners and teachers?

Acquiring Essential Knowledge

Open Educational Resources are teaching, learning, and research materials in any medium that reside in the public domain or have been released under an open license that permits no-cost access, use, adaptation, and redistribution by others.[10] Or we could use this less technical definition to describe OER: OER are educational materials that can be freely downloaded, edited, and shared to better serve all students.[11]

OER and Open Textbooks
To begin, you should watch the video *Why OER?*
https://www.youtube.com/watch?v=qc2ovlU9Ndk | CC BY 3.0

In contrast to traditional educational materials, which are constantly becoming more expensive and less flexible, OER give everyone, everywhere, free permission to download, edit, and share them with others. David Wiley provides another popular definition, stating that only educational materials licensed in a manner that provides the public with permission to engage in the 5R activities can be considered OER.

The 5R permissions are:

1. *Retain*—permission to make, own, and control copies of the content (e.g., download, duplicate, store, and manage it)
2. *Reuse*—permission to use the content in a wide range of ways (e.g., in a class, in a study group, on a website, in a video)
3. *Revise*—permission to adapt, adjust, modify, or alter the content itself (e.g., translate the content into another language)

4. *Remix*—permission to combine the original or revised content with other material to create something new (e.g., incorporate the content into a mashup)
5. *Redistribute*—permission to share copies of the original content, your revisions, or your remixes with others (e.g., give a copy to a friend)

The easiest way to confirm that an educational resource is an "open" one that provides you with the 5R permissions is to determine that the resource is either in the public domain or has been licensed under a Creative Commons license which permits the creation of derivative works; these licenses are CC BY, CC BY-SA, CC BY-NC, and CC BY-NC-SA.

Open educational resources come in all shapes and sizes. An OER can be as small as a single article, academic paper, video, or simulation, or it can be as large as an entire degree program. However, it can be difficult, or at least time-consuming for teachers to assemble OER into a collection that is comprehensive enough to replace an "all rights reserved" copyrighted textbook. When OER are collected and presented in ways that resemble a traditional textbook, it often makes it easier for teachers to use the resources. The term open textbook simply means a collection of OER that has been organized to look like a traditional textbook in order to ease the adoption process. To see examples of open textbooks in a number of disciplines, visit OpenStax (licensed CC BY 4.0, available at http://openstaxcollege.org/), the Open Textbook Library (licensed CC BY 4.0, available at https://open.umn.edu/opentextbooks/), or the BC Open Textbook Project (licensed CC BY 4.0, available at https://open.bccampus.ca/). Other times, OER are aggregated and presented as digital courseware. To see examples of open courseware, visit the Open Education Consortium (licensed CC BY 4.0, available at http://www.oeconsortium.org/courses/) and MIT Open-CourseWare (licensed CC BY-NC-SA 4.0, available at https://ocw.mit.edu/index.htm).

In addition to demonstrating that learners save money when their teachers adopt OER, research shows that learners can have better outcomes when their teachers choose OER instead of educational materials that are available under "all rights reserved" copyright.

The use of OER is strongly advocated by a broad range of individuals, organizations, and governments, as evidenced by documents like the Cape Town Open Education Declaration (2007), the UNESCO Paris OER Declaration (2012), and the recently adopted UNESCO Ljubljana OER Action Plan (2017).

	Cost to Students	Permissions for Faculty and Students
Commercial Textbooks	Expensive	Restrictive
"The Web" MOOCs Library Resources	"Free"	Restrictive
Open Educational Resources	Free	5Rs

FIGURE 5.3
OER-Enabled Pedagogy, slide 16

Figure available at https:// www.slideshare.net/ opencontent
Author: David Wiley
CC BY 4.0
Desaturated from original

OER vs. Free Library Resources

Teachers and professors typically use a mix of "all rights reserved" commercial content, free library resources, and OER in their courses. While the library resources are "free" to the learners and faculty at that institution, they are (1) not really "free" because the institution's library had to pay to purchase or subscribe to them, and (2) they are not available to the general public. The chart in figure 5.3 describes the cost to learners and the legal permissions available to teachers and learners for each of these types of educational resources.

OER in Primary and Secondary (K–12) Education vs. Tertiary (Higher) Education

Open educational resources are used in all sectors of education. How OER are produced and adopted, however, often differs depending on the level of education in which they are used.

In general, tertiary (higher education) faculty members are more likely to:

- have the time, resources, and support to produce and revise educational resources;
- own the copyright to the content they create (though this depends on their contract with the college or university); and
- make unilateral decisions regarding what content is used in their courses.

As such, higher education faculty are often OER producers and can decide whether or not to adopt these OER in their courses. OER adoption in higher education tends to occur one faculty member at a time. Given this opportunity, it is critical that faculty members be given the time, resources, and support they need in order to create and adopt open education content and undertake a shift to open education practices and pedagogy. For an example of this sort of endeavor, see the open textbook Clinical Procedures for Safer Patient Care that was written by faculty from British Columbia (licensed CC BY 4.0 at https://opentextbc.ca/clinicalskills/).

In general, primary and secondary (K-12) teachers are less likely to:

- have the time, resources, and support to produce and revise educational resources;
- own the copyright to the content they create (though this depends on their contract with the school or district); and
- make unilateral decisions regarding what content is used in their curriculum.

As such, OER adoption in primary and secondary schools tends to occur at the district or school level, rather than at the level of individual teachers. For an example of this, see the blog post Creative Commons policies grow in New Zealand schools (https://creativecommons.org/2014/10/06/creative-commons-policies-grow-in-new-zealand-schools/).

Open Educational Resources (a very brief timeline)

While there isn't enough space in this section to give a comprehensive overview of the "History of Open Education," here are several of the pivotal events that contributed to the growth of the Open Education movement.

- 1969: UK Open University opens
- 1983: Free software movement founded with launch of GNU
- 1991: World Wide Web becomes publicly available
- 1997: MERLOT project begins
- 1998: U.S. Copyright Term Extension Act
- 1998: The term *open content* is coined, and the Open Content License is released
- 1999: Open Publication License is released
- 1999: Connexions launches (renamed OpenStax in 2012)
- 2001: *Wikipedia* is founded
- 2001: Creative Commons is founded
- 2001: MIT Open CourseWare is established

- 2002: Budapest Open Access Initiative
- 2002: Creative Commons licenses launched
- 2002: UNESCO coins the term Open Educational Resources
- 2004: First annual Open Education Conference
- 2005: OpenCourseWare Consortium is formed (renamed the Open Education Consortium in 2014)
- 2006: WikiEducator is launched
- 2007: Cape Town OER Declaration
- 2007: OER Commons is established
- 2007: Wiley and Couros experiment with "open courses"
- 2008: The book Opening Up Education is published
- 2008: The online course "Connectivism and Connective Knowledge" is established; 2,000 learners participate, leading to the term *massive open online course*, or MOOC
- 2012: OpenStax releases the first open textbook
- 2012: UNESCO OER Paris Declaration
- 2013: OERu (Open Educational Resources university) is launched
- 2017: UNESCO 2nd World OER Congress
- 2018: UNESCO drafts an OER Recommendation
- 2019: UNESCO approves bringing 2019 UNESCO OER Recommendation to the next General Conference.

Final Remarks

OER, whether organized as open textbooks or open courseware, provide teachers, learners, and others with a broad range of permissions that make education more affordable and more flexible. These permissions also enable rapid, low-cost experimentation and innovation, as educators seek to maximize access to effective educational resources for all.

5.4 | FINDING, EVALUATING, AND ADAPTING RESOURCES

We live in a rich multimedia culture that requires educators to provide relevant learning resources in the classroom, although finding and reusing others' great works is not always simple. This section will teach you how to find others' OER and adapt them for use in your own classroom.

FIGURE 5.4 **Cell phone**

Photo from Unsplash:
https://unsplash.com/
photos/E1XoOa77f5U
Author: Tiago Aguiar
Public domain: CC0
Destaurated from original

Librarians play an important role in the discovery, development, description, licensing, curation, and sharing of Open Educational Resources. They also have an opportunity to advocate for and support the use of these resources. This section will also guide you through a practical approach to supporting the adoption of OER.

THE BIG QUESTION: WHY IT MATTERS

What skills and knowledge are needed to find just the right OER that you and your learners need? If you are going to join the global Open Education community, find the best open resources for your course, and share your good work as an OER, you need to know—and know how to teach others—how to find, evaluate, and adapt openly licensed resources. And what if we want to think bigger . . . what effect might Open Education have globally?

Why is the openness of content—the ability to revise, remix, and share it—so important? If the public had access to and could creatively remix the world's knowledge, what new opportunities might we find to address global challenges (e.g., the United Nations Sustainable Development Goals)?

LEARNING OUTCOMES

- Find OER in open repositories, or by using Google, CC Search, or other platforms
- Evaluate how to reuse, revise, and remix the OER you find
- Demonstrate how different OER can be used together, while paying attention to license compatibility

PERSONAL REFLECTION: WHY IT MATTERS TO YOU

Where do you currently find your learning resources? Do you seek open alternatives for the materials you currently use? How do you evaluate your existing learning resources, and how can you apply those measures to openly licensed content?

Once you identify the learning resources you currently use, ask yourself the following questions:

- Is this resource freely available to all of my learners?
- Can my learners and I keep a copy of this resource forever?
- Does my class have the legal rights to fix errors, update old or inaccurate content, improve the work, and share it with other educators around the world?
- Can my learners contribute to and improve our learning resources as part of their course work?

If the answer to these questions is "No," then you're probably using learning resources that don't provide the legal permissions you and your learners need to do what you want to do. Conversely, if you answered "Yes" to all of the questions, then you're probably using OER.

Acquiring Essential Knowledge

FINDING RESOURCES

Not everything on the Internet is an open educational resource, and some works labeled as "open" may not have the legal permissions to exercise the 5Rs. So how do you recognize OER, and how do you choose which OER will work best in your class?

 First, for a short introduction on how to find OER, watch the video How Can I Find OER? **https://www.youtube.com/watch ?v=NJRIaQkiWKw** | CC BY NC 4.0

Finding the resources you want to use is the first step to bringing OER into your classroom. Discovery is one of the primary barriers for educators who want to use OER. Fortunately, there are many established ways to search for these resources.

You can do a quick review of OER projects and people on the OER World Map (licensed CC BY 4.0 at https://oerworldmap.org/) to get a sense of global OER activities.

There are many websites that host large collections of OER (e.g., Wikimedia Commons), but some universities also host their own OER repositories and services. A good first step is to do a general OER search using Google Advanced Search and filter your results by "Usage Rights" (on the pull-down menu at the bottom of the screen). See Google's post on how to use the tool effectively at https://googleblog.blogspot.com/2009/07/find-creative-commons-images-with -image.html.

In addition to sharing your OER on your website or blog, there are hundreds of online platforms on which you can share your openly licensed content. Creative Commons maintains a directory of some of the most popular platforms used by educators, organized by content type (photos, video, audio, textbooks, courses, etc.) at https://creativecommons.org/about/program-areas/education -oer/education-oer-resources/. You can also find OER on these platforms.

When looking for OER, open educators often ask each other for help on Open Education discussion lists. Here is a non-exhaustive tally of discussion lists you might be interested in joining:

- CC Open Education Platform (invitation)
- OER Forum
- International OER Advocacy
- OER Discuss
- Open Knowledge Open Edu
- Open Edu SIG
- Wikimedia Education
- US OER Advocacy
- SPARC: Library OER
- Educause Openness

If you want to know more about the most popular general options for searching for OER, read the Open Washington course Module 6: Finding OER (licensed CC BY 4.0 at http://www.openwa.org/module-6-2/).

Creative Commons redesigned its CC Search (figure 5.5).[12] You can explore the initial version of the new search engine (images only) at https://ccsearch .creativecommons.org. Soon, CC Search will be able to search the entire Commons—all of the public domain and CC-licensed works on the Internet . . . including OER.

FIGURE 5.5 **CC Search**

EVALUATING RESOURCES

As with all education resources, OER need to be evaluated before use. Educators who are new to OER may have concerns about their quality because these resources are available for free and may have been remixed by other educators. But the process of using and evaluating OER is not that different from evaluating traditional "all rights reserved" copyright resources. Whether education materials are openly licensed or closed, you are the best judge of quality because you know what your learners need and what your curriculum demands.

Subject specialists (educators and librarians) assess the quality and suitability of learning resources. The membership organization JISC provides a list of criteria for the assessment of the quality of these resources.

- Accuracy
- Reputation of author/institution
- Standard of technical production
- Accessibility
- Fitness for purpose[13]

You should be careful not to let anyone tell you that OER are "low quality" because they are free. As the SPARC OER Mythbusting Guide points out:

- In this increasingly digital and Internet-connected world, the old adage that "you get what you pay for" is growing outdated. New models are developing across all aspects of society that dramatically reduce or eliminate costs to users, and this kind of innovation has spread to educational resources.

- OER publishers have worked to ensure the quality of their resources. Many open textbooks are created within rigorous editorial and peer-review guidelines, and many OER repositories allow faculty to review (and see others' reviews of) the material. There is also a growing body of evidence which demonstrates that OER can be both free of cost and high quality—and more importantly, they can support positive student learning outcomes.[14]

Also, be careful not to get pulled into a debate about high- or low-quality educational resources when what educators should really be concerned about is those resources' effectiveness. Read these two posts from David Wiley: "Stop Saying 'High Quality'" (https://opencontent.org/blog/archives/3821) and "No, Really—Stop Saying 'High Quality'" (https://opencontent.org/blog/archives/3830).

Remixing and Adapting Resources

Being open enables educators to use the resource more effectively, which can lead to better learning and student outcomes. OER can be remixed, adapted, updated, or tailored and improved locally to fit the needs of learners—for example, by translating the OER into a local language, adapting a biology open textbook to align it with local science standards, or modifying an OER simulation to make it accessible for a student who cannot hear.

The ideas of remixing and adaptation are fundamental to education. The creative reuse of materials created by other educators and authors is about more than just seeking inspiration; we copy, adapt, and combine different materials in order to craft appropriate and effective education resources for our learners.

Incorporating materials created by others and combining materials from different sources can be tricky, not only from a pedagogical perspective, but also from a copyright perspective.

Online digital education resources have different legal permissions that empower (or not) the public to use, remix, and share those resources. Here are a few of those legal categories:

- Public domain works (which are not restricted by any copyright) can be remixed with any other work.
  - » *Example:* Anyone can remix *The Adventures of Huckleberry Finn* by Mark Twain with *Alice's Adventures in Wonderland* by Lewis Carroll.
- Some "all rights reserved" copyrighted works are available for free online, but you can only use them under the project terms of service,

or by using an exception or limitation to copyright, such as fair use or fair dealing.

>> *Example:* Many MOOCs allow free reuse of their content, but do not allow copying, revise, remix, or redistribution.

- "All rights reserved" copyrighted works in closed formats do not allow the public to remix or adapt the work.

  >> *Example:* A blockbuster movie is usually available only on a streaming service that you cannot use or even link to.

- Creative Commons-licensed works (and other free licenses) are open, but they may have various permissions and restrictions.

  >> *Example:* The online encyclopedia *Wikipedia* (BY-SA) allows you to reuse its content for commercial purposes, while WikiHow (BY-NC-SA) does not. A *Wikipedia* article cannot be remixed with a WikiHow article.

If you want to know which CC-licensed works can be remixed with other CC-licensed works, see figure 5.6, which repeats the CC remix chart (figure 4.12) that we studied in chapter 4. In this chart, where there is a check mark at the intersection of two CC-licensed works, you can remix those two works. Where there is a black X, you cannot remix those two CC-licensed works.

MARC Records and Metadata

There are metadata standards for OER that allow searchability, organization, and integration into current content systems at your institution. Metadata can include information such as author, title, subject area, grade level, keywords, and other categorical information.

There are many sources whereby you can easily include open textbooks in your library collection. UnGlue.it has a comprehensive database of Creative Commons ebooks. In 2014 they added 1,897 free ebooks, and of these, 1,076 of them have Creative Commons licenses. Unglue.it has also added librarian tools (https://unglue.it/accounts/edit/marc_config/) to allow users to download and upload customizable MARC (machine-readable cataloging) records. As free, openly licensed resources, OER often live outside of the catalog, and cataloging standards can differ between repositories. You can check out the WorldCat catalog record for OpenStax to see what an OER might look like in the catalog

	PUBLIC DOMAIN	PUBLIC DOMAIN	CC BY	CC BY-SA	CC BY-NC	CC BY-ND	CC BY-NC-SA	CC BY-NC-ND
PUBLIC DOMAIN	✓	✓	✓	✓	✓	✗	✓	✗
PUBLIC DOMAIN	✓	✓	✓	✓	✓	✗	✓	✗
CC BY	✓	✓	✓	✓	✓	✗	✓	✗
CC BY-SA	✓	✓	✓	✓	✗	✗	✗	✗
CC BY-NC	✓	✓	✓	✗	✓	✗	✓	✗
CC BY-ND	✗	✗	✗	✗	✗	✗	✗	✗
CC BY-NC-SA	✓	✓	✓	✗	✓	✗	✓	✗
CC BY-NC-ND	✗	✗	✗	✗	✗	✗	✗	✗

FIGURE 5.6 **CC License Compatibility Chart**

Figure from Creative Commons: https://creativecommons.org/faq/#can-i-combine-material -under-different-creative-commons-licenses-in-my-work
CC BY 4.0 | Desaturated from original

(https://www.worldcat.org/title/openstax/oclc/824454682). How do you catalog OER? If you're participating in the CC Certificate course, use the class chat to discuss this question.

The Open Textbook Library and BC Campus also provide MARC bibliographic records for OER. The Open Textbook Library also uses CC0 for all of its MARC records. You can read more about how to use CC for MARC records at http://dltj.org/article/cc0-marc-records/.

Final Remarks

We live in an amazing world of information abundance, and an increasing percentage of our digital knowledge is openly licensed. But finding the right open resources that fit the needs of your learning spaces and your learners can be a challenge. One of the major motivations for using OER is the ability to revise, remix, and share these works in ways that will best suit the needs of your learners. Search engines, OER repositories, and platform services with built-in tools for using Creative Commons licenses help, but finding the right OER can still take time for your faculty and library patrons to accomplish.

5.5 | CREATING AND SHARING OER

Large parts of this book are about creation, both how it works from a legal perspective and, more practically, how we learn by making and creating something. In this section we will explore and practice how to create and share OER so they can have the biggest impact and be used without any legal or technical barriers.

THE BIG QUESTION: WHY IT MATTERS

A big part of any educator's work is preparing, updating, and combining learning materials. Making those materials open requires just a few additional steps, and it's easier than you think. What are those steps? What should you consider and expect when you want to create and publish your resources in the open?

When we share our education resources as OER, we share our best practices, our expertise, our challenges and solutions. Education is about sharing. And when we share our work with more people, we become better educators.

LEARNING OUTCOMES

- Imagine how your OER will work in practice
- Understand how to select CC licenses for your resources
- Examine your open license decision for compatibility (i.e., can it be remixed) with other OER
- Identify the needs and challenges to improving OER accessibility for everyone

Personal Reflection: Why It Matters To You

What kind of learning resources do you create now? Do you publish or share these resources with other people for feedback? Which of your resources do you think could benefit fellow educators, learners, researchers, and libraries? If you choose to share, how much freedom do you want to give to others; in other words, what permissions will you allow for others to reuse your work?

For an introduction on why it is important to share your work as an OER, watch the video *Open Education Matters: Why Is It Important to Share Content?* **https://www.youtube.com/watch?v=dTNnxPcY49Q** | CC BY 3.0

Acquiring Essential Knowledge

WHY SHARE?

Because educators and librarians can share OER with everyone for near zero cost,[15] we should do this. After all, education is fundamentally about sharing knowledge and ideas. Libraries are about archiving, sharing, and helping learners to find the knowledge they seek. When we CC-license our work, we are sharing that work with the public under simple, legal permissions. Sharing your work is a gift to the world.

CHOOSING A CC LICENSE FOR OER

As you may remember, not all educational materials that are available under a CC license are OER. Review the chart in figure 5.7 that details which CC licenses work well for education resources and which do not.

The two CC NoDerivatives (ND) licenses are not OER-compatible licenses because they don't allow the public to revise or remix the educational resource. Because the ND licenses do not meet the 5Rs or any of the major OER definitions, the Open Education movement does not consider ND-licensed educational resources to be "OER."

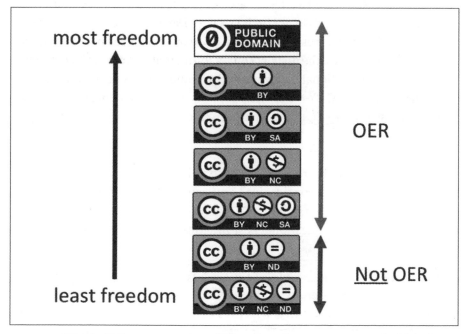

FIGURE 5.7 **Which CC licenses work well for education resources and which do not**

Choosing the right license for your OER requires you to think about which permissions you want to give to other users—and which permissions you want to retain for yourself. Read the statement "Open Textbook Community Advocates CC BY License for Open Textbooks" (licensed CC BY 4.0 at https://open .bccampus.ca/2016/11/04/open-textbook-community-advocates-cc-by-license -for-open-textbooks/) and think about why they recommend the Creative Commons Attribution license (CC BY) for education. You can find more arguments made about the utility of this same license for publishing scientific research in the article "Why CC BY?" from the Open Access Scholarly Publishers Association (licensed CC BY 4.0 at https://oaspa.org/why-cc-by/).

For basic information about the licenses, and how to choose and apply one to your work or to combined works from other people and sources, revisit section 4.1 "Choosing and Applying a CC License."

CC LICENSE LEGAL CASES IN OPEN EDUCATION

For a detailed analysis of Creative Commons case law, see section 3.4 "License Enforceability." Creative Commons maintains a listing of court decisions and case law from jurisdictions around the world on its wiki, licensed CC BY 4.0 at https://wiki.creativecommons.org/wiki/Case_Law.

In 2017–18 there were two legal cases concerning Open Education: *Great Minds vs. FedEx Office* and *Great Minds vs. Office Depot*, as referenced in chapter 4. As a reminder, both cases involved OER used by schools for non-commercial purposes. In both cases, the district courts found that a commercial copy shop may reproduce educational materials at the request of a school district that is using them under a CC BY-NC-SA license; thus, no license copyright infringement or violation of the CC license had occurred.

OTHER CONSIDERATIONS

Other than choosing the right CC license, what other aspects of openness and pedagogy are worth considering? You can read a list of best practices to include in your work when building OER at https://maricopa.instructure.com/ courses/805732/pages/educational-best-practices?module_item_id=5139807.

Watch the video *Simply Said: Understanding Accessibility in Digital Learning Materials* by the National Center on Accessible Educational Materials. **https://www.youtube.com/watch?v=HzE5dj1WTSo**

FIGURE 5.8 **Print encyclopedia and e-book reader on green grass**

Photo from Pixabay: https://pixabay.com/en/e-reader-e-book-ebook-e-ink-1213214/
Author: papirontul | Public Domain: CC0 | Cropped and desaturated from original

The Open Washington network's Module 8 on "Sharing OER" (licensed CC BY 4.0, available at http://www.openwa.org/module-8/) will give you practical advice on how to share OER online and prepare them to be used offline as well.

ENSURING THAT OER ARE ACCESSIBLE TO EVERYONE

At its core, OER are about making sure that everyone has access to learning and research materials. Not just rich people, not just people who can see or hear, not just people who can read English—everyone.

As authors and institutions build and share OER, best practices in accessibility need to be part of their instructional and technical design from the start. Educators have legal and ethical responsibilities to ensure that our learning resources are fully accessible to all learners, including those with disabilities.

The best practices to ensure that your OER are accessible to all include:

- putting your work into the public domain (CC0) or adding a non-ND CC license to your work;
- making it simple to download your work in editable file formats, so others can modify or translate it to meet local needs and make it accessible; and
- most importantly, designing your work to be accessible from the start.

LIBRARY WEBSITES, LIBRARY SUBJECT GUIDES, CATALOGING, AND CREATIVE COMMONS

Librarians who find themselves in the role of content creators may wonder how to license their work. Over 5,000 institutions in the United States use LibGuides as their preferred subject guide content management system, with over 120,000 license holders around the world. Licensing your resources under Creative Commons can be as simple as using the license chooser to create a machine-readable icon for your site or LibGuide.

There are hundreds of LibGuides on library websites about Creative Commons alone. Use Google to search for LibGuides about Creative Commons and flip through the resources found by subject librarians on the issues of Creative Commons and copyright.

Final Remarks

Openness in education means more than just access or legal certainty over what you are able to use, modify, and share with your learners. Open Education means designing content and practices which will ensure that everyone can actively participate and contribute to the sum of all human knowledge. As educators and learners revise others' OER and create and share new OER, accessibility should always be on your design checklist.

5.6 | OPENING UP YOUR INSTITUTION

This section discusses how educational institutions can support open education content, practices, and community with policy.

THE BIG QUESTION: WHY IT MATTERS

Educational institutions around the world are trying to figure out how to support their educators, staff, and learners in using, revising, and sharing OER in the context of new Open Education practices. How can educational leaders use various policy tools to support and promote Open Education?

LEARNING OUTCOMES
- Consider if and why you need a policy to accomplish your Open Education goals
- Understand the menu of Open Education policy options
- Assess your existing institutional policies
- Understand how to develop an institutional open policy

PERSONAL REFLECTION: WHY IT MATTERS TO YOU
What if there were institutional policies that supported your Open Education and open access efforts? What effect might pro-Open Access and pro-Open Education policies have on you and your learners?

Acquiring Essential Knowledge
Educational institutions have a broad menu of Open Education policy options from which to choose. Your institution can:

- Raise awareness of the existence of OER and their benefits for your learners and faculty.
  - » *Action:* Host an annual "Open Education" day at your school or university.

- Empower stakeholders to drive your institution's Open Education strategy.
  - » *Action:* Create an Open Education Task Force comprised of learners, faculty, accessibility experts, deans, bookstore, financial aid, and library staff, instructional designers, eLearning, and so on.

- Ensure that all of the content you fund is OER.
  - » *Action:* Draft, adopt, and implement an open licensing policy requiring university or school-funded resources to be openly licensed (preferably CC BY 4.0). Use the OER Policy Development Tool (licensed CC BY 4.0, available at http://policy.lumenlearning .com/) to build an open policy for your institution. You can find examples of open policies that others have created at the OER Policy Registry (global; licensed CC BY 4.0, available at https:// wiki.creativecommons.org/wiki/OER_Policy_Registry) and SPARC's "List of North American OER Policies and Projects" (licensed CC BY 4.0, available at https://sparcopen.org/our-work/list-of-oer -policies-projects/).

- Issue a call-to-action to solve an educational challenge.
  - » *Action:* Create an OER grant program. You could appropriate funds for supporting faculty and staff to shift your fifty highest-enrolled courses from closed content to OER.
    - *Example:* The Maricopa County Community College started an open textbook initiative to lower the costs of teaching materials. They provided grants to create open courses and train faculty on OER. You can learn more about their process at https:// maricopa.instructure.com/courses/811971.

- Leverage existing strategic documents to support Open Education.
  - » *Action:* Add Open Education goals to your institution's key strategy documents.
  - » *Action:* Identify and track key performance indicators that improve when courses and/or degrees adopt OER.
    - *Example:* Increasing student outcomes, increasing the percentage of learners who can access 100 percent of the learning resources on day 1, reducing dropouts during add/drop periods, increasing credits taken per semester, decreasing student debt, decreasing time to degree.

- Make it easy to share OER.
  - » *Action:* Join a global OER repository and make it simple for your educators and learners to find others' OER and share their own OER. Provide professional development.

- Ensure that educators have the legal rights to share.
  - » *Action:* Change the contract between the institution and the faculty or teachers so that these educators have the legal rights to CC-license their work.
    - *Example:* A Creative Commons policy in New Zealand gives teachers advance permission to disseminate their resources online for sharing and reuse. The policy also ensures that both the school and the teacher—as well as teachers from around the country and around the world—can continue to use and adapt resources produced by New Zealand teachers in the course of their employment. Creative Commons NZ has developed an annotated policy template for schools to adapt (http://resources .creativecommons.org.nz/cc-schools-policy/).

- Provide OER information to learners.
  - » *Action:* Require OER Course designations in course catalogs so learners can see whether (or not) a course uses an OER or an open textbook.
    - *Example:* The City University of New York labels OER in its catalog; see the video. **https://www.youtube.com/watch?v=jRjTRza_l18 &feature=youtu.be**.

- Reward sharing.
  - » *Action:* Adjust promotion and tenure policies to reward the creation, adoption, and maintenance of OER and publishing in Open Access journals. The creation and adaptation of OER should be appropriately recognized as curricular innovation and service to the academic profession during promotion and tenure review.

ENFORCING OPEN EDUCATION AND OPEN ACCESS POLICIES

The point of most Open Education and Open Access policies is to ensure that publicly (or foundation) funded education and research resources (1) can be read by everyone, (2) are openly licensed, and (3) are shared in editable file formats in public repositories, with a zero embargo period, which provides immediate public access upon publication. Creative Commons often uses the catchphrase "publicly funded resources should be openly licensed resources—the public should have access to what it funds." When it comes to enforcing Open Education and Open Access policies, multiple people and institutions play important roles.

Government, foundation, and institutional funders and program officers responsible for managing grants and contracts need to (1) understand their Open Education/Access policies, (2) communicate the importance of these policies to grantees verbally and in writing, and (3) check to ensure that the public has full access to the openly licensed resources, research, and data under the terms of the Open Education and Open Access policy.

University or college administration should provide support (e.g., by hiring a full-time OA or OER librarian) to faculty who are publishing in Open Access journals or otherwise sharing their research openly and to faculty who are creating, remixing, sharing, and adopting OER. Institutions should also review and modify (as needed) promotion and tenure policies to ensure that faculty who are engaged in Open Education and Open Access publishing are rewarded during promotion and tenure review.[16]

Final Remarks

When educational institutions support their educators, staff, and learners in moving from closed to open content and practices, Open Education thrives. Educators want to design the best courses, adjust their practices and pedagogy to empower learners to co-create knowledge, and push the limits of knowledge by openly sharing their ideas and resources with a global audience. But educators can't do it alone. They need political, financial, time, staff, and policy support to shift to, and fully realize, the benefits of Open Education.

5.7 | ADDITIONAL RESOURCES
More Background on Open Access

- "A Very Brief Introduction to Open Access," by Peter Suber.
  This is a short description defining Open Access, research articles, Open Access repositories, archives, and journals: http://api.ning.com/files/JOi7zGa2fuzuS*bGstF4DkFDsquoaB8WAHtxNzkKpmGEJcUtvb ArAaUG56hLkiZaT3jSnZf354VW573zjj25qhlUnRcN6POA/Averybrief introductiontoOpenAccessA4.pdf.

- "Open Access Overview," by the University of Minnesota Libraries.
  This is an introduction to Open Access, and specifically how it pertains to librarians. It also provides additional resources and information from SPARC about open access for librarians: https://www.lib.umn.edu/openaccess/open-access-overview.

- "Open Access Publishing: A New Model Based on Centuries of Tradition," by the University of Washington Libraries.
  This is a brief introduction to Open Access publishing for librarians, and includes supplementary links to related guides for librarians regarding open access support: http://guides.lib.uw.edu/research/spoa.

- "Open Access Publishing," by Berkeley Library Scholarly Communication Services.
  This provides information on open access, funding, and how open access scholarship fits into the framework of academic publishing: http://www.lib.berkeley.edu/scholarly-communication/publishing/open-access-publishing.

- "HowOpenIsIt? A Guide for Evaluating the Openness of Journals," by SPARC in conjunction with PLOS and the Open Access Scholarly Publishers Association.
  Presented as a downloadable chart, this guide provides a means to identify the core components of open access and how they are implemented across the spectrum between "open access" and "closed access": https://sparcopen.org/our-work/howopenisit/.

- "Academic Libraries and Open Access," by Aaron Tay.
  This is a substantial discussion regarding how Open Access publishing fits into the space of academic publishing at large, and the current issues surrounding Open Access: https://medium.com/a-academic -librarians-thoughts-on-open-access/academic-libraries-in-a-mixed -open-access-paywall-world-can-we-substitute-open-access-for-d30fa 182cafd.

- "Removing the Barriers to Research: An Introduction to Open Access for Librarians," by Peter Suber.
  This article is a detailed description of Open Access for librarians that digs into some of the deeper logistics of how Open Access publishing works in practice: https://legacy.earlham.edu/~peters/writing/acrl.htm.

- "Open Access: The True Cost of Science Publishing," by Richard Van Noorden.
  This article discusses the ethics of publishing, including how Open Access quells some of these ethical issues, and the practicality of free access to journals: https://www.nature.com/news/open-access-the-true -cost-of-science-publishing-1.12676.

- "We've Failed: Pirate Black Open Access Is Trumping Green and Gold and We Must Change Our Approach," by Toby Green.
  This discusses current issues in the realm of Open Access publishing and offers prescriptions for how to make improvements to current models: http://onlinelibrary.wiley.com/doi/10.1002/leap.1116/full.

- "Open Access Overview: Focusing on Open Access to Peer-Reviewed Research Articles and Their Preprints," by Peter Suber. CC BY 3.0.
  This article provides definitions, initiatives, and discussion surrounding Open Access, including discussions regarding journals, repositories, cost models, and the public interest: https://legacy.earlham.edu/ ~peters/fos/overview.htm.

- "Is the Staggeringly Profitable Business of Scientific Publishing Bad for Science?" by Stephen Buranyi.
  This article discusses the ethics of the traditional academic publishing model and its impact on the propagation of new research and scientific discoveries: https://www.theguardian.com/science/2017/jun/27/ profitable-business-scientific-publishing-bad-for-science.

- "Understanding Open Access: When, Why, and How to Make Your Work Openly Accessible," by Lexi Rubow, Rachael Shen, and Brianna Schofield at the Samuelson Law, Technology, and Public Policy Clinic. CC BY 4.0.
  This is an in-depth overview of Open Access and how to make your own work openly accessible: https://authorsalliance.org/wp-content/uploads/Documents/Guides/Authors%20Alliance%20-%20Understanding%20Open%20Access.pdf.

More Information about Open Access and OER Advocacy

- ROARMAP: *Registry of Open Access Repository Mandates and Policies,* by the School of Electronics and Computer Science at the University of Southampton.
  This is a searchable international registry of existing Open Access policies, including their terms and details: http://roarmap.eprints.org/981/.

- "OER and Advocacy: What Can Librarians Do?" by the University of Toronto Libraries.
  This contains resources and information on how librarians can support OER adoption, and it also provides some faculty perspectives on OER: https://guides.library.utoronto.ca/c.php?g=448614&p=3199145.

- "Scholarly Communication Toolkit: Scholarly Communication Overview," by the Association of College & Research Libraries.
  This is a toolkit to help librarians integrate a scholarly communication perspective into library operations and programs, as well as prepare presentations on scholarly communication issues for administrators, faculty, staff, students, and other librarians: http://acrl.libguides.com/scholcomm/toolkit/.

More Information about Emerging Models of Open Access Publishing

- "Open in Order to . . . Accelerate Research and Scientific Discoveries," by Timothy Vollmer. CC BY 4.0.
  This is an article about the value of Open Access based on a recap of a Creative Commons Slack chat about the importance of preprints for Open Access publishing: https://creativecommons.org/2017/10/25/open-order-accelerate-research-scientific-discoveries/.

- "Q&A with PLOS Cofounder Michael Eisen," by Richard Poynder. This is an interview with Michael Eisen about the costs and future of Open Access publishing: https://poynder.blogspot.ca/2017/10/q-with -plos-co-founder-michael-eisen.html.

NOTES

1. Martha Kyrillidou and Mark Young, eds., *ARL Statistics 2002-03* (Washington, D.C.: Association of Research Libraries, 2004), table 2, http://www.libqual.org/ documents/admin/2012/ARL_Stats/2002-03arlstats.pdf.

2. Peter Suber, "Open Access Overview: Focusing on Open Access to Peer-reviewed Research Articles and Their Preprints," Earlham College, June 21, 2004, revised December 5, 2015, https://legacy.earlham.edu/~peters/fos/overview.htm.

3. Currently, the Termination of Transfer tool covers U.S. copyright and contracts controlled by U.S. law only. Creative Commons is working to expand the tool to provide information and resources about provisions with similar effect around the world.

4. The SCAE and the addenda are being updated by Creative Commons in 2018.

5. Éric Archambault, Grégoire Côté, Brooke Struck and Matthieu Voorons, *Research Impact of Paywalled Versus Open Access Papers*, (Quebec, Canada: Science-Metrix and 1Science, 2016) http://www.1science.com/1numbr/.

6. "Open-access Mandate," *Wikipedia,* last edited March 22, 2019, https://en.wikipedia .org/wiki/Open-access_mandate.

7. National Institutes of Health, "Public Access Policy," https://publicaccess.nih.gov/ policy.htm.

8. Most OER are "born" digital, though they can be made available to learners in both digital and printed formats. Of course, digital OER are easier to share, modify, and redistribute, but being digital is not what makes something an OER or not.

9. While in many countries (such as many EU member states) cost may not be a problem, restrictive copyright and narrow fair use and fair dealing rights can limit new teaching methods.

10. This is a Creative Commons adaptation of the UNESCO OER definition: http:// www.unesco.org/new/en/communication-and-information/access-to-knowledge/ open-educational-resources.

11. Drafted by OER Comms, which is a coalition of North American open education advocates working on OER communication: oer-comms@googlegroups.com.

12. Creative Commons' existing Search tool is at https://search.creativecommons.org.

13. "Quality Considerations," PBWorks, https://openeducationalresources.pbworks .com/w/page/24838164/Quality%20considerations.

14. SPARC, OER *Mythbusting*, (Washington, D.C.: SPARC, 2017), https://sparcopen.org/ our-work/oer-mythbusting/.

15. While in many EU member states and some other countries cost may not be a problem, restrictive copyright and narrow fair use and fair dealing rights can limit new teaching methods.

16. See Oklahoma State University's Provost & Senior Vice President of Academic Affairs declaration of support in the promotion and tenure process for faculty working with OER: https://www.youtube.com/watch?v=Jh2qmNm9gcQ&feature =youtu.be.

Index